MANZANO

IMMIGRANT COMMUNITIES & ETHNIC MINORITIES IN THE UNITED STATES & CANADA: No. 34

ISSN 0749-5951

Series Editor: Robert J. Theodoratus
Department of Anthropology, Colorado State University

1. James G. Chadney. *The Sikhs of Vancouver.*
2. Paul Driben. *We Are Metis: The Ethnography of a Halfbreed Community in Northern Alberta.*
3. A. Michael Colfer. *Morality, Kindred, and Ethnic Boundary: A Study of the Oregon Old Believers.*
4. Nanciellen Davis. *Ethnicity and Ethnic Group Persistance in an Acadian Village in Maritime Canada.*
5. Juli Ellen Skansie. *Death Is for All: Death and Death-Related Beliefs of Rural Spanish-Americans.*
6. Robert Mark Kamen. *Growing Up Hasidic: Education and Socialization in the Bobover Hasidic Community.*
7. Liucija Baskauskas. *An Urban Enclave: Lithuanian Refugees in Los Angeles.*
8. Manuel Alers-Montalvo. *The Puerto Rican Migrants of New York City.*
9. Wayne Wheeler. *An Analysis of Social Change in a Swedish-Immigrant Community: The Case of Lindsborg, Kansas.*
10. Edwin B. Almirol. *Ethnic Identity and Social Negotiation: A Study of a Filipino Community in California.*
11. Stanford Neil Gerber. *Russkoya Celo: The Ethnography of a Russian-American Community.*
12. Peter Paul Jonitis. *The Acculturation of the Lithuanians of Chester, Pennsylvania.*
13. Irene Isabel Blea. *Bessemer: A Sociological Perspective of a Chicano Bario.*
14. Dorothy Ann Gilbert. *Recent Portuguese Immigrants to Fall River, Massachusetts: An Analysis of Relative Economic Success.*
15. Jeffrey Lynn Eighmy. *Mennonite Architecture: Diachronic Evidence for Rapid Diffusion in Rural Communities.*
16. Elizabeth Kathleen Briody. *Household Labor Patterns among Mexican Americans in South Texas: Buscando Trabajo Seguro.*
17. Karen L. S. Muir. *The Strongest Part of the Family: A Study of Lao Refugee Women in Columbus, Ohio.*
18. Judith A. Nagate. *Continuity and Change Among the Old Order Amish of Illinois.*
19. Mary G. Harris. *Cholas: Latino Girls and Gangs.*
20. Rebecca B. Aiken. *Montreal Chinese Property Ownership and Occupational Change, 1881—1981.*
21. Peter Vasiliadis. *Dangerous Truths: Interethnic Competition in a Northeastern Ontario Goldmining Community.*
22. Bruce La Brack. *The Sikhs of Northern California, 1904—1975: A Socio—Historical Study.*
23. Jenny K. Phillips. *Symbol, Myth, and Rhetoric: The Politics of Culture in an Armenian-American Population.*
24. Stacy G. H. Yap. *Gather Your Strength, Sisters: The Emerging Role of Chinese Women Community Workers.*
25. Phyllis Cancilla Martinelli. *Ethnicity In The Sunbelt: Italian-American Migrants in Scottsdale, Arizona.*
26. Dennis L. Nagi. *The Albanian-American Odyssey: A Pilot Study of the Albanian Community of Boston, Massachusetts.*
27. Shirley Ewart. *Cornish Mining Families of Grass Valley, California.*
28. Marilyn Preheim Rose. *On the Move: A Study of Migration and Ethnic Persistence among Mennonites from East Freeman, South Dakota.*
29. Richard H. Thompson. *Toronto's Chinatown: The Changing Social Organization of an Ethnic Community.*
30. Bernard Wong. *Patronage, Brokerage, Entrepreneurship and the Chinese Community of New York.*

Continued at back of book

MANZANO

A Study of Community Disorganization

Wesley R. Hurt

AMS Press, Inc.
New York

AUTHOR'S NOTE

This study is based upon a thesis with the same name submitted to the Sociology Department, University of New Mexico, 1941, to meet the requirements for a Masters Degree. Paul A. F. Walter, Jr. served as the chairman of my committee.

The original work has been revised by adding additional material, eliminating redundant data, and reorganizing the text.

I wish to acknowledge the aid of Merle E. Simmons in translating the portions of the text written in Spanish. Mary C. Hurt performed an invaluable service in editing the text.

Library of Congress Cataloging-in-Publication Data

Hurt, Wesley R. (Wesley Robert), 1917-
    Manzano : a study of community disorganization.
    p. cm. — (Immigrant communities & ethnic minorities in the United States & Canada ; 34)
    Bibliography: p.
    Includes index.
    ISBN 0-404-19444-3
    1. Community organization—New Mexico—Manzano. 2. Social institutions—New Mexico—Manzano. 3. Manzano (N.M.)—Social conditions.
    I. Title. II. Series.
    HN80.M23H87   1989
    306'.09789'63   88-35132

AMS PRESS
56 East 13th Street
New York, N.Y. 10003, U.S.A.

MANUFACTURED IN THE UNITED STATES OF AMERICA

CONTENTS

LIST OF ILLUSTRATIONS

CHAPTER I

INTRODUCTION

Introductory Statement

Since the onset of the world-wide depression in 1929, people of the United States have begun to realize that many communities are in a serious state of disorganization. Elliot and Merrill cite two examples of this condition,

> "Centerville is a mill town which to outward appearances has made a good recovery since the depression. Men are back to work, industrial output is good, wages are adequate, relief loads are low. But Centerville lacks coordinating forces because of political corruption, religious conflict, and factional strife...
>
> "Community disorganization applies more spectacularly to Megalopolis. Megalopolis is a city badly disrupted by economic distress, political corruption, and crime...The depression came and people literally had no money for a two years' tax accumulation. Teachers' salaries went unpaid for months." (1941:787)

Sanchez lucidly describes disintegration and decline of Spanish-American civilization in New Mexico in these words,

> "Neglected for more than two hundred years as Spanish colonial and Mexicans, their cultural situation was not greatly improved by the territorial regime. In fact, the little improvement that took place through the educational efforts that were made in their behalf was more than offset by the social and economic decline that resulted from the influx of new peoples and a new economic order." (1940:27)

Organization of communities forms the central theme of Steiner's studies of American cities and villages (1928). The Lynds describe many features of conflicts in a typical American community (1929). The fact that so many communities are in this condition suggests that a program

of social reconstruction must be found. Before such course can be

followed, however, the many factors contributing to the condition must

be discovered. A program to rehabilitate a community divided by labor

unions and political factions could not be applied to one in which

disruption of institutions and mores is the cause. Not all social

scientists would agree that it is necessary to find a program of

reconstruction for a disorganized community. According to Cuber,

> Traditionally, under the dominance of the cyclical hypothesis,
> disorganization has been thought of as a pathological condition
> antecedent to disintegration, but much current disorganization
> seems to be a normal process by which institutions are rationally
> adapted to changing conditions." (1938:403-413).

Objective of This Study

It is the objective of this study to depict the cultural history of

a community, Manzano, New Mexico, that is now entering a state of

serious disorganization, in particular, in its economic system. By using

the cultural-historical method, it is often possible to find forces in a

community which may have contributed to its disorganization. For

example, if it is found that a breakdown of institutions is followed by

a state of confusion in a society, it can be suggested that disruption

of institutions was a causal factor in the later disorganization of the

community. Since the community is composed of many interrelated cultural

and social factors, it can not be suggested that the breakdown of

institutions was the sole cause of disorganization, but only one of many

factors. Therefore, it is necessary to depict as many aspects of the

cultural history of a community as are still available in the written

records and in the memory of the inhabitants. If the causes of a

particular community's disorganization are found, the first step in reconstruction has been accomplished. If the community's problems are similar to those of other societies, a broader and more important series of causal factors has been uncovered. Thus, the importance of an intensive investigation of the cultural history of one community is established.

Concepts and Definitions

Community

Sociologists have viewed the concept of "community" from two related points of view: the geographical and the psychological. Consequently, many definitions have been advanced. Wirth defines a community as including, "A territorial base, distribution in space of men, institutions, and activities, close living together on the basis of kinship and organic interdependence, and a common life based upon the mutual correspondence of interests." (1933:61-73). Park and Burgess define the concept as follows: "Community is the term which is applied to societies and social groups where they are considered from the point of view of geographical distribution of the individuals and the institutions of which they are composed." (1924:161)

The fact that a community does not have a definite geographical boundary but depends upon what aspect of life is being considered has been recognized by Kolb and Brunner. They state,

> "It is the fusing of the geographical or ecological and psychological or functional elements which gives the community idea its real power and usefulness. To follow this in analysis is not always easy, for unlike the village, the town or rural community does not have such an easily recognizable physical base or a definite corporate boundary". (1940:113)

In connection with the investigation of the village of Manzano, it is necessary to redefine the concept to the following: the community of

Manzano includes those Spanish-American inhabitants living in the
Manzano voting precinct and sharing common group life. Spanish-
Americans refers to the native born peoples who are Spanish in descent,
although the Manzaneños refer to themselves as "Mexicans". In this sense
they are contrasted with the Anglo-Americans whose native language is
English and who are of northern European descent, although some live in
Manzano.

Community disorganization

According to Cuber, disorganization is a concept applied by many
sociologists to a number of social phenomena (1938:408-413). Other
writers object to its usage because it seems to have an inherent value
connotation. Yet disorganization as applied to institutions appears to
be objectively measurable in terms of (1) declining participation by the
rank and file, (2) confusion among functionaries, and experimentation in
Modus operandi (1938:408-413).

Elliot and Merrill have well characterized the nature of community
disorganization as follows:

> "The vitality and effective functioning of a community are
> dependent upon harmonious cooperative efforts and consensus of
> social definition, in agreement as to general ends and purposes.
> When this common definition is translated into cooperative
> activity toward some common end, we have community efficiency.
>
> "When the local citizens cease to be concerned with their
> community welfare, the social structure of the community is
> threatened...When a sizable segment of the community puts its
> economic interest, its religious sectarianism, or its own pleasure
> above the welfare of the group, community disorganization is
> imminent." (1941:791)

An important factor in the disorganization of a community is the
amount of participation of the component individuals. According to

Elliot and Merrill, "Community organization and disorganization are thus direct functions of the activities of the citizens and their participation in community and civic affairs." (1941) The lack of interest in community participation has been expressed by Lynd, "Now, thank God, I don't have to know my neighbors, go to Rotary, belong to a church, or participate in an annual Community Chest drive." (1939:83) Individual participation in a community is, however, a relative matter, for every individual enters in the life of a community to a certain extent. Elliot and Merrill have classified individuals according to type of participation (1941:783). The first category is those persons with no definite group or institutional connections in the community; the second group includes those who are members of definite organized institutions which are not in themselves functionally integrated into the community. The third group is those who participate fully in the integrated community institutions.

Processes of Community Disorganization

The processes of individual, family, and community disorganization are not static or unrelated to each other but form integrated, dynamic components of a whole. In other words, parts of a system. Thus, the breakdown of any one factor is detrimental to the others. Because of the dynamic character of community life, certain of the components may change more rapidly than others and result in confusion; this is especially true of communities in contact with other cultural groups. Social scientists disagree among themselves as to the end result of community disorganization. Some adhere to the belief that disorganization may have more destructive features than positive (Elliot and Merrill 1941:797).

That there is a slow but eventual amelioration of society out of the
confused transitional stages of disorganization has been noted by
Burgess (1925:54).

Role of Institutions in Community Organization

As was suggested previously, the well being of a community is
highly dependent upon institutional organization. According to Summer,
an institution is a concept plus a structure. An institution is
basically an idea, notion, interest, or purpose which provides the
motivating force for the development of some mechanism for carrying out
this self-same idea, notion, or interest (1906). Summer also states,
"The structure is the framework or apparatus or perhaps only a number of
functionaries set to cooperate in prescribed ways at a certain
conjecture." (1906:53)

According to Chapin, local social institutions arise from repeated
groups of interacting human individuals in response to elementary needs
or drives. Out of these needs, a structure is developed which consists
in a combination of four related types. The resulting configuration
possesses relative rigidity and relative persistence of form and tends
to function as a unit of contemporary culture. These type parts
of a structure are (1) attitudes or behavior patterns; (2) symbolic
culture traits or symbol; (3) utilitarian culture traits or property;
(4) codes or written specifications. The type parts may be illustrated
in the family: (1) underlying attitudes and behavior patterns of love,
affection, loyalty, and respect; (2) the marriage ring, family crest,
and heirlooms are symbolic traits; (3) the home and furniture are
utilitarian traits; (4) the marriage license, the marriage certificates,

family practices, and genealogy and (5) oral and written codes (1935:Chapter II).

Institutions tend gradually to become forces of conservatism in a community and eventually become an end instead of a means. Elliot and Merrill have cited the example of respect for the flag becoming more important than good government. Eventually these institutions become over-aged and atrophy. As a result, they are an important factor in the community (1941:800).

Methods of Investigation

The research was initiated at Manzano in June, 1938, when I was employed by the Museum of New Mexico on an archaeological project at the nearby Abó ruins. During the summer of 1938, I lived at the Civilian Conservation Camp in Canyon Colorado [Red Canyon], some six miles southwest of Manzano, where I spent evenings and week-ends interviewing the natives of Manzano. In November, 1938, I was transferred to the Kuaua ruins near Bernalillo, New Mexico. Research at Manzano was resumed in January, 1939, when I was transferred to the nearby Quarai ruins as project supervisor of the Works Projects Administration under the co-sponsorship of the Museum of New Mexico. At the Quarai restoration and excavation project between 10 and 30 men from Manzano and Punta de Agua were constantly employed, thus enabling me to obtain information on this project without always resorting to the formal interviews. This position also enabled me to obtain invitations to various activities at Manzano. Research at the communities of Manzano, Punta de Agua, Chato, Torreón, Tajique, and Chilili was carried on simultaneously from January, 1939, to August, 1940.

Informal   interviews and participant-observation were the two
techniques, however, that were used the most in conducting the research
in the villages. Kluckhohn gives the   justification for the latter
technique as, "The use of the technique will provide a desirable balance
between   purely behavioristic type of investigation and the type which
seeks some measure of insight into the 'meanings current in the
community.'" (1940:331) Nearly all the interviews with the non-English-
speaking informants were carried out in Spanish.   When possible,
nevertheless, I preferred to use English with those informants who could
speak this language fluently for it reduced the possibility of
misinterpretation. This constraint excluded nearly all individuals over
60 years of age since most of them could not speak sufficient English.
An additional technique was to collect autobiographies from the older
informants and excerpts from some of these are presented in the text and
in the Appendices.

Further information was gathered from the files of various county,
state and federal   offices in Estancia, Santa Fe and Albuquerque.
Valuable information was gathered about the early period of American
acculturation from the Gringo and Greaser, a newspaper published at
Manzano in 1884 and from the files of the Estancia News Letter, a
newspaper still in circulation and published in Estancia, New Mexico,
the county seat. Further information was obtained by interviewing Anglo-
Americans and local Syrians who lived in Manzano, rural areas of
Torrance County as well as in Mountainair, New Mexico. Data from the U.
S. Census, several books on Spanish-American culture, such as Sanchez's
Forgotten People, Walter's, The Cities That Died of Fear, Barker's
Caballeros,   and   the Conservation Economic Series of the Soil
Conservation Service at Albuquerque were also utilized.

Geographical Setting and Natural Resources of the Manzano Area

Manzano, the "town of the apple orchard", is located on the east slope of the Manzano Mountains and the west side of the Estancia Valley in New Mexico (Figures I and III). For sheer beauty of setting, there are few rivals among the other towns in the state, if not in the Southwest. Whether approached from the north or the east, the picturesqueness of Manzano justifies the sixty-five mile trip from Albuquerque, the nearest large center of population. To the west rise the green pine-forested Manzano Mountains to an elevation of 10,000 feet while several miles to the east lies the large, grass-covered basin of the Estancia Valley, the site of a great Pleistocene lake and the present-day location of several small towns and villages, as well as a series of salt pans. According to Meinzer, the lake at its greatest extent covered 450 square miles, with a maximum depth of almost 150 feet. It stood at its highest level about 15,000 years ago (1911:310).

A more detailed description of the region was made by Bailey. In reference to the Manzano Mountains and surrounding area he states,

> "The Canadian Zone covers the tops of these mountains and the cold slopes down to about 8,000 feet. It is well marked by a rather meager forest of white fir, blue spruce, Douglas spruce, Pinus flexilis, aspen, and Rocky Mountain maple, with mountain ash, alders and willows in cold gulches and along streams...The Transition Zone covers the greater part of the mountains from approximately 7,000 to 8,000 feet on cold slopes and 8,000 to 9,000 feet on warm slopes. On the east side of the range it spreads out over a wide area of gently sloping ridges and mellow-soiled valleys, well clothed with open pine forests, scattered oaks of the Quercus gambeli, New Mexico locust, and low undergrowth of Ceanothus fenleri... and many Rocky Mountain plants...
>
> "The Upper Sonoran Zone of the foothills and surrounding valley is the main zone of agriculture and stock raising. The foothill division of this zone is of particular interest along the eastern slope of the mountains, where it carries picturesque little forest of nut pines, juniper, and scrub oaks, with tree cactus, prickly pear, yuccas, red barberry, skunk brush...and other shrubs...Much

if not most of this juniper belt would seem admirably adapted to apples if sufficient moisture for the growth of trees and fruit could by proper cultivation be conserved in the soil. The natural growth of gramma grass and other grasses is good and forms fine grazing while the gulches and timber afford good shelter for stock." (1913: 69-70)

The village itself lies at an elevation of 7,000 feet on the ecotone of the Transition and the Upper Sonoran Life Zones. Because of a short growing season in the Transition Zone Manzano lies at the upper margin of agriculture. Beside the large spring on the southwest corner of the settlement (Figure IV) is a lone pine while around the village are cottonwoods, pinons, junipers, oak and salt cedar. The main border of the pine forest begins on the west about a mile upslope and three miles to the north. A few pines scattered in the intervening area indicate that the forest may have extended at one time much lower. The trees of the Upper Sonoran Zone extend downslope along an arroyo for about three miles into the Estancia Valley, from which the grasslands cover the plains for hundreds of miles eastward. The Estancia Valley is suitable for dry farming during years of normal moisture but because of frequent droughts the only lands that can produce crops consistently are those that have access to irrigation from streams and artesian wells.

The following is a reconstruction of the crop yields in Manzano of the last decade:

1928 - a year of poor crops with less than 100 pound sack of beans per acre.
1929 - an ordinary year for crops.
1930 - good crop yield.
1931 - good crop yield.
1932 - drought, crop failure.
1933 - drought, crop failure.
1934 - an ordinary year for crops.
1935 - winter came early with an eight inch snow on September 27th. Snow did not ruin the beans which had an ordinary yield of five sacks per acre.
1936 - a severe freeze occurred which killed all the growing beans. Yield of beans was two sacks per acre.
1937 - snowed in the mountains until June 5th and freezing in Manzano.

This forced the crops to be planted very late. A drought followed and the yield was only one sack of beans per acre.

1938 – severe winter with deep snow; frost began on October 20; almost complete crop failure.

1939 – heavy snow and rainfall; arroyos that usually were dry had running water until mid summer; highest crop yield in the decade.

The main part of Manzano lies between two arroyos (Figure III). The arroyo on the north carries water only during the spring or after heavy rains while the south arroyo normally would have water flowing throughout the year if it were not diverted for irrigation from its source, the permanent spring, Ojo del Gigante [Spring of the Giant], that lies at the southwest corner of the town. On the south arroyo there is also a large reservoir with an earthen dam. Other parts of Manzano lie on the slope of the hill to the south of the reservoir and several houses are built along the highway that runs from Manzano to Chato.

The nearest community to Manzano, Chato, is located about two miles south of Manzano on an unsurfaced road winding into Canyon Colorado [Red Canyon]. This village is a small settlement of farmers who depend upon Manzano for their marketing, entertainment, and religious activities. The next nearest town is Punta de Agua, five miles southeast on the highway leading to Mountainair. While Punta de Agua is in the Manzano Land Grant, the inhabitants trade in the local stores or in Mountainair and attend religious services in the local church. Mountainair, a major regional trade center, lies 16 miles to the southeast and is the source of much cultural influence on the three communities. The Manzaneños (the Spanish method of designating the inhabitants of Manzano) visiting Mountainair become familiar with American inventions, movies, modes of living, etc. in addition to engaging in a large volume of buying and selling. The telephone line from Estancia to Mountainair passes through Manzano. There is, however, only one telephone at Manzano, the one at

Tabet's store. Mail is delivered daily by truck from Mountainair and is distributed in this store.

Twelve miles north, on the highway from Manzano to Albuquerque, lies Torreón, the nearest settlement in this direction. Although Manzano and Torreón have active communication with one another, mainly through the medium of family visiting and public dances and fiestas, their cultural influence on each other is limited. A few miles beyond Torreón, on the same highway, is Tajique, whose influence on Manzano is even less. The most distant community on this highway that might be considered in active communication with Manzano, with the exception of Albuquerque, is Chilili. With Chilili the relation is chiefly intermarriage and social visits.

About 30 miles to the northwest of Manzano is Estancia, the county seat of Torrance County. Communication is active between this town and Manzano, principally for political and governmental business. Although Albuquerque, the largest city in New Mexico, is only 65 miles to the northwest and connected by a good highway, it has little direct influence on the culture of Manzano but some communication is carried on between these two communities by business firms and governmental agencies and by tourists. Three roads lead to Manzano but during severe winters the town becomes snowbound frequently and also isolation occurs because of impassable roads during heavy summer rains.

The most important natural resources of Torrance County are 249,666 acres of National Forest, 974,904 acres of grasslands and 66,874 acres of woodland pasture (U. S. Census, Agriculture, 1930:42). Although these resources are potentially important for timber and grazing, the county income depends largely upon dry farming. Normal precipitation throughout the region is approximately 14 inches (Works Projects Administration 1939:10).

On the east and south slope of the Manzano Mountains are several abandoned mines whose exploitation is no longer profitable. The Scholle district, on the south side, produced $324,143 in gold, silver, and copper between 1915 and 1930. (Lasky and Wooton 1933:117,118, 122). In the region between Mountainair and Scholle there are gypsum deposits, a mineral used by the Spanish-Americans to make haspe [whitewash]. Sulphur is obtained in small quantities in the county and a small amount of salt is gathered from the saline lakes. Although these lakes are no longer important, they were for centuries one of the main sources of salt for Indians and Spanish-Americans of New Mexico. A few traces of coal outcrop in the mountains in the northwest section of the county although the beds are not mined (Works Projects Administration 1939:10).

The Spanish-American Communities of New Mexico

The Spanish-American communities of New Mexico furnish a fertile field for investigation of community disorganization. Originally they were subjects of Spain but after the Treaty of Cordova signed in 1821 they became citizens of Mexico and so remained until New Mexico became territory of the United States after the bloodless conquest by Stephen W. Kearny 1846. The capital and seat of the legislature was Santa Fe. At the time Manzano was settled in the early part of the nineteenth century it was under the direct administration of Don Jacinto Sanchez, president of the Ayuntamiento [town council] of Tomé in the central Rio Grande Valley. Local authority for law and justice was an appointed official, the alcalde. This official had the power of inflicting corporal punishment or incarceration but since Manzano had no jail the latter punishment was not inflicted. At Manzano a pioneer alcalde still remembered was Miguel Lucero.

The New Mexican villages during the Spanish and Mexican regimes were relatively isolated politically and economically, their major contact being with an antagonistic people, the American Indians. During this period, from A.D. 1600 to 1800 the Spanish-American culture continued to be acculturated with that of the Indians, a process that began in Mexico. This acculturation, however, was very selective since the Spanish-Americans incorporated mainly those traits and objects of material culture which aided in their survival, i.e. articles of food, tools, and agricultural practices. Traits such as indigenous religion which would have been very disruptive to their culture organization were not adopted. Institutions such as the peon-patrón system and the Catholic Church united the people internally into one compact body, with everyone having and fulfilling a place in the society. Further integration was achieved by the highly organized militia to protect against Indian raids, the institution of Water Commissioners to control the maintenance of irrigation canals and dams and the allocation of water, and the Land Grant Commissioners who allocated land to petitioners.

After New Mexico was conquered in 1846 and became a Territory of the United States in 1848 by the Treaty of Guadalupe Hildalgo the influence of Anglo-American culture began to be felt by the Spanish-American communities. It was more than a mere influx of new ideas and cultural traits, for the natives in some towns were almost replaced by Anglo-Americans. Other towns such as Santa Fe became almost evenly divided in population composition. In such communities the Spanish-American culture became highly assimilated with that of the Anglo-

Americans. In contrast in the small, isolated mountain and desert communities many aspects of Spanish-American culture have survived even though there are at present many indications of their rapid disintegration. This is exemplified in the progressive disappearance of native folklore, customs, mores, agricultural and other economic practices and institutions such as the Penitente religious cult. Furthermore, the fact that from 20 - 50% of the Spanish-Americans in these isolated communities are being compelled to ask for state and governmental economic relief suggests that their cultural autonomy is breaking down.

Walter, Jr. describes the plight of the Spanish-Americans in New Mexico in these words,

> "The story of the Spanish-speaking communities of New Mexico is that of a people who, in isolation from the rest of the world, found an adjustment to their physical environment and resources which served as a comfortable and secure way of life for three hundred years; and then in a single generation have seen the bases of that adjustment swept out from under them. A quarter million of these people now face the pressing need of adapting themselves to the new conditions for which they are but poorly equipped by their customs and traditions. They must make a sweeping cultural readjustment, it appears, with little or no outside aid, and they are notably lacking in initiative and self-reliance. It is a crisis which has descended upon them with such startling rapidity that there is not yet sufficient perspective for a complete appraisal." (1939:150)

On the basis of their income the communities which still retain much of the Spanish-American culture fall into several classes. One, of which Galisteo is an example, has an economy based upon livestock raising. Cedro of Tijeras Canyon is typical of another type of village which has an income based upon livestock raising, a minute amount of agriculture, and the hauling and selling of firewood to Albuquerque. In Tijeras Canyon area $23,000 of the total cash income was derived from the sale of wood (United States Department of Agriculture 1937C:4). San José is another variety where the income is derived mainly from employment in

the Santa Fe Railroad shops and other industries of the adjacent city of
Albuquerque. The largest number of Spanish-American communities in New
Mexico, however, are those which depend upon subsistence agriculture and
small scale grazing operations.

Because the agricultural villages form the largest group of
Spanish-American communities in New Mexico, Manzano was selected as a
representative site for the study of community disorganization. A
preliminary survey was made in the Spanish-American villages of the
Estancia Valley because all are included in the state and federal relief
programs, all have evidence of cultural loss, and yet have preserved
much of their native culture. These villages are all characterized by an
economy based upon dry and irrigation farming plus livestock raising.
For example, Sanchez states in reference to the livelihood of Spanish-
Americans, that this economy is, and always has been, based on a bare
subsistence agriculture and small scale grazing operations (1940:9).
Manzano was selected because it lay nearest to my place of residence,
with the exception of the much smaller village of Punta de Agua, but
also because it still had many old people who could give information on
data not available in written records. In other communities such as
Chilili, Torreón, and Tajique, a preliminary survey revealed many less
elderly people.

Description of the Settlement Pattern of Manzano

Manzano is built around a plaza in typical Spanish-American style
with the main highway passing through the center (Figure III). On the
west side are situated the only business establishments of the village,
Candelaria's general store, Tabet's general store, Tabet's cantina
[saloon] and a small grocery store owned by another Tabet. On this side

also are several houses while on the north side is the church (Figure VI) and several more houses. On the northwest corner of the plaza is the long, picturesque, red-colored convento (Figure VII) and at the southwest corner is a large cement-plastered building, originally serving as a schoolhouse and now used for a dance hall.

South of the main part of the settlement is the large earthen dam and lake (Figure IX). Still further on the highway to Mountainair, is located the old gray torreón, a circular watchtower incorporated into an ancient fort with a patio in the center, structures which were built to protect the town from the marauding Navajos and other enemy Indian tribes (Figure VIII). A little beyond the town is a relatively recent apple orchard enclosed by a limestone boulder wall. Continuing south along the highway is the south arroyo which carries runoff from the lake and beyond the arroyo stands the modern red sandstone school house, built in 1938 (Figure V). Adjacent are several large galvanized-iron-roofed houses, shaded by large cottonwood and oak trees.

The large spring, Ojo del Gigante [Spring of the Giant], (Figure IV) is reached by a small winding dirt road lying along the north side of the lake and which then turns west over a hill for about 200 yards. Along the road is the oldest apple orchard, the ruins of an unfinished limestone jail, and a cement-sided tank which contains water for livestock. Many houses and other orchards lie along this road. A road also leads from the livestock tank to a group of houses on a hill that overlooks the impounded lake on the south. This group of houses is locally called El Cerro.

Built on a hillside overlooking on the main settlement on the west is another group of dwellings, while on top of the hill is the ruin of an old morada, the chapel of the Penitentes, abandoned in the latter part of the last century. Few houses are located to the north of the plaza and most of these are on the graveled road that leads to Capillo Peak Lookout Station in the Manzano Mountains. The communal graveyard (Figure IX) and a limestone kiln lie to the west of this road. On the northern margin of the village is the site of an artificial lake bed, the Tanque de la Joya, abandoned about 45 years ago and now planted with peach trees.

While most of the fields utilized for agriculture are in the area surrounding the village, nearly all the orchards and vegetable gardens are within the village and its immediate outskirts, giving the appearance of a typical rural settlement. Livestock roam at will through its rutted and sometimes muddy streets. Walls and outhouses are within view of the highway; in the backyards are corrals and barns. Ditches meander throughout the area. The local people are usually congregated in front of the stores. Fences around houses are less common than in the larger New Mexican cities, while lawns are absent. Few attempts are made to beautify yards with flowers but those that have them are pleasing in appearance. Abundance of wild trees compensate for the lack of cultivated trees.

Historical Setting of the Region of Manzano

Manzano lies within the region known to early Spanish chroniclers as the "Salinas Province", which was a center of the Catholic missionaries' efforts to christianize the Indians. Coronado's expedition in 1540 apparently missed the Salinas Pueblos, the Indian villages near Manzano. Padre Rodriguez and the soldier, Chamuscado, on their return to the Rio Grande Valley in 1581 passed near the salt lakes east of Manzano. Whether they passed through the site of Manzano is not known but they may have gone by the nearby pueblo of Quarai. Somewhere in the vicinity Fray Juan de Santa Maria, one of the priests who accompanied the Rodriguez expedition, was killed by the Maguas Indians. According to Reed, the expedition of Espejo in 1583 probably visited only the Pueblo of Abó, which is about 18 miles west of Mountainair (1940:10). The expedition of Juan de Oñate in 1598 visited the pueblos of Quarai and Abó (Reed 1940:1-9).

The first missionary work in the Salinas province was in 1598 by Fray Francisco de San Miguel, a chaplain of Oñate's army who ministered to the pueblos of Quarai, Abó, and Tabirá from his headquarters at Pecos. In the summer of 1629 Fray Francisco de Acevedo went to the Salinas area and began construction of the large mission churches at Abó, Tabirá, and Quarai (Reed 1940). Apparently no mission was established in the vicinity of the site of Manzano, although Bandelier reports that he heard of several prehistoric sites in the immediate area (Lange and Riley 1966). I found, however, within Manzano and the vicinity projectile points, pot sherds and isolated house sites indicating that Indian farm houses were locally present. In addition, there is the ruins of a small Indian village near the old spring of Manzano, about two miles east of the village.

It has been generally believed and reported that the oldest apple orchard at Manzano was planted by the Spanish missionaries at Quarai Pueblo. For example Bandelier dates this orchard as older than 1675 (Lange and Riley 1966:386). Hawley who investigated this orchard states, "By a study of the growth rings of the apple trees we have discovered that the trees were planted no earlier than 1800 ." (1936:16) Such a date would place the planting during the first years after Manzano was settled. It may be that the present trees are shoots or seedlings from an earlier orchard, of which the original trees died out. Nevertheless, it does not seem logical that the padres at Quarai would plant an apple orchard in this region with its permanent water supply since the area was too open to attack by the Apaches and other Plains Indians. According to older inhabitants of Manzano, the Navajo Indians, when on a raid, camped in the nearby foothills. This fact, perhaps, explains why Manzano itself was not founded before the nineteenth century,

The Quarai mission was occupied for about 45 years in the interval from 1629 to 1674. The mission of Tabirá evidently was abandoned in 1669 while Abó was abandoned about the same time as Quarai (Reed 1940:21-22). It is also reported that frequent raids by the Apaches and other nomadic Indians forced the evacuation of these peaceful pueblos. From then until the founding of Manzano the region was occupied only by marauding Indians.

CHAPTER II

THE FOUNDING OF MANZANO

Although I know of no written records describing the first settlement of Manzano I obtained a description of this event from a local informant, 94 years old, whose grandfather told him this story. In the last of the eighteenth or early part of the nineteenth century, people from Tomé, a village in the Rio Grande Valley north of Belen, settled around a spring on the property of Rafael Garcia about a mile east of the present village of Manzano. This settlement was not large judging by the ruins near the spring. In the ruins some of the people from present day Manzano excavated several human skeletons, a copper button with an incised star, fragments of pottery which are reported to be the type made by people of Manzano, and a black pottery jar. According to the informant, because of the exposed nature of the settlement, the inhabitants were soon driven out by nomadic Indians and returned to Tomé.

There are several unconfirmed reports regarding the next settlement at Manzano. A current story told in the Estancia Valley is that the first settlers were convicts from Spain who were given a land grant there. This report is very dubious considering that in 1829 inhabitants of Manzano petitioned to the Mexican government as free citizens for a land grant. The other common story, that Manzano was colonized by people from La Joya, seems more likely as indicated in the written records of the Land Grant Petition.

21

Until the Mexican Revolution in 1821, New Mexico was a territory of
Spain and after that date became part of Mexico. The first documentary
record that I could find regarding Manzano is in the Grant Petition of
of 1829, made by José Manuel Truxillo and 75 others of Manzano before
Governor Don Bartolome Baca and presented to the Territorial Assembly
(Ayuntamiento) of Tome on September 22, 1929 (Appendix I), according to
a copy of the Grant Petition and accompanying documents taken from the
files of the Manzano Land Grant Commission. An abstract of this petition
can be found also in Twitchell (1914:119-120).

From this petition it is evident that Manzano was actually settled
prior to 1829, when it numbered 160 people. Two of the original land
owners were Colonel Bartolome Baca, governor of New Mexico from 1823-
1825 and Don Antonio José Otero, later appointed circuit judge by
General Stephen W. Kearny, after New Mexico became a territory of the
United States. This petition describes one of the bases of Manzano's
social and economic system, that of granting free land to its
inhabitants. It specified also that "A person who will not reside in the
town with the family belonging to him and who shall remove to another
settlement shall lose all right that he may have acquired to his
property." This restriction prevented for a time outsiders gaining
control of the land. It is also noted in the petition that the village
has a right to exact communal labor from the grantees, a regulation that
still exists at Manzano. The petition mentions that permission was
granted for construction of a mission church but no reference was made
to the apple orchard.

The next record is the Notice of Tomé, September 25, 1829, by José
Manuel Truxillo. This was a petition referred to the Territorial
Deputation by the president of the Ayuntamiento, Don Jacinto Sanchez,

with the statement, "The only objection found regarding the arable land therein situated belonging to the retired Colonel Baca, who will be satisfied with the lands which he as a new settler may acquire; together with that which he has purchased from other settlers, promising that although he will not establish his residence there, he will cultivate and improve the lands which may be recognized as his." A league of land in each direction was granted to the people of Manzano by the Territorial Deputation, of which Antonio Chavez was president and Roman Abreu, secretary. When possession was given, the center was established at "El Alto del Pino de la Virgen " situated in the middle of the cultivated fields. This notice apparently refers to the hill to the east of Manzano.

Espinosa and Chavez have added this information on Governor Bartolome Baca,

"Governor Bartolome Baca established his reputation ? in the early 1800s. Bartolome Baca served as Governor of New Mexico from 1823 to 1825. He served as the third governor under Mexican rule. Governor Baca also served as Captain of the militia for Rio Abajo and at one time served as Alcalde of Tome and Belen in the early 1800s. Governor Baca also acquired large holdings of land on the east side of the Manzano Mountains, known as the Estancia Valley. It is estimated that at one time the land grant of Baca on the east side of the mountains contained over a million acres, his pastured his large flock of sheep and herds of cattle and horses (No date:95).

CHAPTER III

MANZANO DURING THE MEXICAN PERIOD

At the time when Manzano was first settled it was part of the territory of Mexico, a period that terminated in 1846 when New Mexico was conquered by General Stephen W. Kearny.

Original Village Plan

From the founding of Manzano until about 1880 raids by the Navajo were frequent. These hostile Indians forced the Manzaneños to organize their village plan and life style for purposes of defense. Some of the precautions taken against the Indians are revealed in the village plan as shown in Figure II. The community was square, built around a central plaza and surrounded by a high wall pierced with loopholes. At the three entrances to the town were heavy wooden gates, two on the north and one on the south where guards were continually stationed. The main part of the village lay to the east and northeast of the reservoir while a fort and torreón [watchtower] (Figure VIII), which are still standing, were located at the southwest corner facing in the direction of probable attack. Generally the houses had flat roofs so that men could station themselves on top when there was a Navajo raid. For additional protection the first church, a rectangular building, was surrounded by a circular wall. Informants vary in their memory of the location of this church, one stating that it faced the plaza in the northeast section of town and another on the west side. Juan Pablo Sedillo claims that it was located in his yard.

At the northwest of the pueblo was another dam and reservoir called the Tanque de la Joya, the dry bed of which is still present. Running along the south and east sides of the town and connecting with the south reservoir was a ditch called the Acequia del Molino [ditch of the mill] which judging by its name once must have had at least one of the old water mills. According to informants there were four mills at one time located on the irrigation ditches that surrounded the town, with two being on the ditch on the west that connected the two reservoirs. Filipe Garcia, who lives about a half mile east of Manzano on the road to Punta de Agua states that the irrigation ditch which runs through his yard had a mill on it at one time. Other informants state that one mill was located along side of the main, the south, reservoir. The mills were round stone buildings using the principle of the undershot wheel. The mills were described in detail in 1846 by Lieutenant Abert (Walter, 1916:19,20). According, to local informants at one time two other mills stood by the south reservoirs and another by the northern one. The entrances to the town were guarded by heavy wooden gates, two on the north and one on the south. About 1872 the last mill was abandoned and the Manzaneños had to haul their corn to Belen for grinding.

The torreón with the accompanying buildings was one of the village's most prominent structures (Figure VIII). The time of construction is unknown but it is believed to be nearly as old as the town itself. A descendent of Filimeno Sanchez, past owner of the fort, reported that the watchtower had been built by Filimeno's father, Tomás Sanchez, who may be the person of that name listed in the Land Grant

Petition. Another informant, however, stated that Filimeno's father came from a town in the Jemez Mountains after Manzano was settled. In addition, neither Lieutenant Abert in 1846 or Major Carleton in 1855 mention this prominent feature in their descriptions of Manzano.

The fort itself was a large rectangular structure with nine rooms built around a plaza with a well in the center. Facing the plaza was a portal [porch]. The gate now standing adjacent to the torreón was originally a small door within the large door leading into the living room of the fort. The tower itself was incorporated in the northwest corner of the fort. According to informants the tower was originally two stories high and had a single fireplace on each floor. Downstairs a small room was partitioned off from the main chamber. Access to the second story was provided by a trap door and ladder. Several windows were cut in the structure at various times, later to be filled in. Several loopholes, still present, pierced the walls. The torreón was photographed in 1885 by Charles Lummis and at that time had a porch fronting the street. The stone walls were plastered and the building was in excellent condition. The windows visible today do not appear in Lummis' photograph. At present the building is in a dilapidated condition with a large part of the walls of the upper floor fallen in as well as the roof. The large vigas supporting the ceiling of the first floor are said to be original while the cross members appear to be relatively new. The fireplaces, trap door, and corner room no longer exist. In places parts of the whitewash still cling to the limestone block walls. Today the lower floor of the tower is utilized for storage while the remaining rooms of the fort have been remodeled and are used as living quarters by a family descended from the original builder.

For protection against the Indians there was a militia [vigilantes] of about 20 men constantly prepared to fight under the command of a capitan, Genebro Aragon. His right hand man was Jesús Trujillo. Another well-remembered vigilante was Juan Cresus. They always kept food and supplies on hand in rolls and leather bags that hung from the roofs. A guard, known as a sereno, always slept on a roof. For their services they received a salary. In most instances the Indian raiders were Navajos, the Mescalero and Jicarilla Apaches being on friendly terms. Whenever a raiding party was sighted approaching Manzano a drum was beaten, church bells rang, and old people and children fled to the fort and plaza, leaving the vigilantes and able-bodied men ready to fight. Because Manzano was so isolated when their supply of bullets ran out or when there was a shortage of rifles they used bows and arrows, lances and sling shots [hondas] for throwing stones. The bows were made of manzanita or jicale wood with a string of cow or goat sinew. They were small, seldom being over four feet long. The arrows were made of ponil wood with a fletching of four turkey feathers and an iron point tied on with threads from the central shaft of a turkey feather. These arrows were held between the thumb and index finger. Bow guards [manjeras] were made of cow hide (Hurt 1939).

An unusual custom, derived by the Manzaneños from the Indians was the scalp taking custom and ceremony. One particular instance of scalping the Indians was told to me by Timio Luna, an informant, a quarter-blood Indian, who lives in La Cienega, a small farming settlement to the south of Manzano. When he was young, he witnessed a group of men from Manzano returning from a fight with Indians near the Sierra Oscura Mountains. Tied to the straps of their saddles were the scalps of many Indians, trailing blood as they rode along. After the scalps were taken to Manzano there was great rejoicing and the scalps were placed on a long pole and carried through town. At night a dance was given to celebrate, a custom that may be related to the Pueblo Indian scalp ceremonies (White 1932:98)

Stories of warfare with the Indians and other types of contact form one of the largest bodies of folklore at Manzano. In addition, these skirmishes with the Indians strengthened the solidarity of the village inhabitants. The contact with the Indians fall into these several types:

1. Joint Manzano and Apache punitive expeditions against the Navajos.

2. Warfare but differing in that of above in that captives were not killed.

3. Raids and reprisals for the purposes of obtaining captives for slavery.

4. Raids to obtain livestock.

5. Friendly contacts.

Manzano was for many years a center of contact with the Apaches, Navajos, and Pueblo Indians, a relationship not always hostile. Pueblo Indians used to go to the salt lakes in the Estancia Valley for their salt (Walter 1916:45). During their travel the Indians from the southern Rio Grande pueblos usually went through Abó Pass, missing Manzano. Those, however, who came from the north occasionally passed through the town and were often friendly.

Many of the people of Manzano and neighboring communities had close friends among members of the different bands of Indians. Juan Archuleta, from Manzano married a woman in Torreón and and moved to that village. He then became the local capitán of the vigilantes. Although he had many Indian friends, he was known, nevertheless, as one of the bravest Indian fighters of Manzano. One of his best friends was El Cadete, chief of one of the Mescalero bands. Once El Cadete and his band raided farms near Torreón, carrying off a large number of livestock. The vigilantes, together with several volunteers, started after the Indians but Juan begged them to stop. He asked that he be permitted to talk with El Cadete, believing in this way he could get the stock back. They consented and he started off alone by muleback. Following their trail over the Manzano Mountains, he came into a deep canyon and approached the Apaches in a camp near the Ojo del Casa. In the darkness El Cadete failed to recognize Archuleta. He lifted his rifle, fired, and Archuleta fell from his mule, dead. The Indians approached the body and when El Cadete saw whom he killed, he began to cry, saying he had killed "Mi hermano" [My brother]. He and his band rode off, sorrowfully.

At Manzano the best Indian fighters were Juan Carillo and Genebro Aragon. One time an Indian caught Carillo near Capulin Canyon in the Manzano Mountains and started to knife him. Aragon killed the Indian and saved his life. The Navajos sometimes raided the area for horses. One story told at Manzano is about Reyes Salas of Torreón who had a very fine horse. He kept it locked at night in a barn with pole windows and a very strong door. One night two Navajos came and cut the poles. One Indian climbed in and found a rope, which they used to saw an opening in the adobe wall to let the horse out.

Other stories regarding problems with the Navajo are remembered at Manzano. Once a woman in Manzano was cooking bread and a Navajo came to the window asking for some. She had a pan full of hot lard and threw it in his face. He ran about 50 feet and died.

One time a large group of Navajos were raiding near Manzano when a large storm came forcing them to flee. One of the warriors fell by the wayside and almost froze to death. He wandered towards Manzano and arrived finally at a house belonging to a grandparent of Lucas Zamora. The inhabitants built a fire and warmed up the Indian. They then bound him with ropes and took him prisoner to the alcalde [justice of the peace]. The alcalde had him bound to a post in the plaza where all could see him. As the news leaked out large numbers of the villagers came and stared at him, shouting and screaming derisively. After that he was taken to Tomé and put in jail.

One time there were 20 Manzaneños guarding a large herd of sheep when a band of about 500 Indians came upon them. A fight ensued and one Indian threw a Manzaneño to the ground and killed him while a villager killed an Indian with a bola. In the fight 5 to 8 Manzaneños were killed and 10 to 15 Indians died, all slain with knives, arrows and bolas. Nevertheless, the Indians won and ran off with the sheep. Another story concerns Felix Salas who lived in a log house, in which he kept a very valuable horse. One time when he fell asleep on the doorstep three Indians came. One slipped through the window and stole the horse. There are also stories about fights between Juan Cisneros and Francisco Sedillo and the Indians.

Some of the Indian bands, in particular the Navajos, were considered enemies and the custom of taking Indian slaves was sanctioned by Spanish law (Bloom and Donnelly 1933:12). For example, Filimeno Sanchez, a local patrón, had from 20 to 30 peones [indentured servants] under his control, among whom were five male and four female Indian slaves, two of which were bought from Gregorio Quintana, their captor. These Indians had all been bought when young from Spanish-American slave raiders and were adopted into the Sanchez family. Their value was about five pesos or the price of a horse. The Spanish-American peones were purchased Indians who had held them captives or were obtained by trading captive

Indian babies for them. Two _peones_ are recalled, one being Juan José Turrieta, the father of Florentino Turrieta who is still living and the father of David Candelaria who is also still alive. The Indian slaves contributed much to the richness of Manzano culture for they were responsible for the introduction of blanket weaving and several other Indian traits.

Intermarriage with slaves appears to have been common. Records show that four of Sanchez's slaves were Navajo men named Eugenio, Manuel, Julian, and Rafael; four were women named Tomasita, Maria, Bartola, and Cruz. Manuel had a son, named Eugenio, by a Spanish-American woman of Manzano. Eugenio married a native of Manzano, Rosa Sanchez, who is still alive. Eugenio died in 1936, the last living of the former Navajo slaves at Manzano. They had ten children, the sons being Juan, Enrique, José, Filimeno and Teodoro; the daughters were Aurora, Rita, Maria and Aguida. One of the sons, Filimeno, was educated at the Apache Indian School on the Mescalero Reservation in New Mexico. He returned and married a Spanish-American women, still alive today. They in turn had three children. Thus, in Manzano three generations of people with mixed blood have resulted from the single marriage of one of Sanchez's Indian slaves. Manuel Sanchez, a full-blooded Indian, was another of Filimeno's slaves who lived with a local women, Isabel Serna, and they had a son, José Serna, who is still living in Manzano. Another full-blooded Indian in Manzano was José Antonio Silva, who retained the Indian custom of wearing long hair with a red band wrapped around it. The father of another man was a half-breed Indian from Las Nutrias. Juan Archuleta brought to Manzano an Indian boy and girl from Quilites, a Indian settlement reported to have existed in the Rio Grande Valley. No record tracing the local descendants of these two Indians was found at Manzano.

Another group of Apache slaves married with village inhabitants; Anamaria was one of the them. Nana Cruz was a half Indian who lived in Manzano. At the age of 25 she was captured by the Navajos. She escaped and returned to Manzano. Later she married a Navajo and went to live with him in Canyon Bonito near Cebolleta. In time she left her husband and went to the Spanish fort at Cebolleta where she remained until a wagon train from Manzano took her back to her home in the village. Cruz Otero was another woman from Manzano who was captured by the Indians. Later they released her and she came back to Manzano to live. Dionicio Molino was a Navajo who was taken captive when young near La Joya. He was later captured by his tribe. After several years he escaped and came back to Punta de Agua where he made his living as a sheepherder.

The patrones still remembered at Manzano are Tomás Sanchez, Filimeno Sanchez, Miguel Lucero, Juan Lucero and Antonio Roble. It is noteworthy that only Tomás Sanchez was included in the list of the original grant petitioners, suggesting that the others were rich men who either came to the village or were born in the village after it was founded. Only one landowner, who employed a group of laborers, is mentioned in this petition, the well-known Governor, Bartolome Baca, not a resident of Manzano. Of the known patrones Fiimeno Sanchez, was the best liked by his peones. The birthplace of Filimeno is unknown but it may have been in Manzano since the name of his father, Tomás, is listed in the names of the Grant Petitioners of 1829 (Appendix I), as mentioned above.

The patrones also engaged in the trading business. It is said that Filimeno Sanchez operated many covered wagons throughout the Southwest hauling and trading supplies. When Manzano was under Mexican rule, he made his fortune trading with Chihuahua City. After the American rule he changed his route to Leavenworth, Kansas, and during the gold rush of 1849, drove large herds of livestock to California.

According to Rosa Sanchez, who married one of Filimeno's Indian slaves, Filimeno, when young played in the torreón, direct evidence that this structure was built by his father, Tomás. The date of Filimeno's death is unknown but Mrs. Sanchez stated that he was already an old man in 1883 when she married. The peones were given a wage, about $3.00 a month. Food and other essentials were issued to them from a general store owned by the patrón. Their hair was clipped close to the scalp to distinguish them from freemen. They labored for the patrón during the day; at night they made their own clothing from wool issued to them by the patrón. The peon-patrón system may be compared with the organization of a large family, the peones representing the children and the patrons representing the parents. Many stories are told at Manzano illustrating the paternal nature of the patrones. For example, one tale relates Sanchez's just treatment of an Indian slave whom he caught stealing. Other informants claim that this was not always true stating that when Filimeno caught a slave or peon stealing he took him to Miguel Lucero, the alcalde, also a patrón. The guilty person was undressed, bound in chains and beaten with two sticks. Another story of stealing from Filimeno states that he hid his money in a box under the doorstep. One of his Indian slaves walking over the step noticed the hollow sound. He pried open the step and found the box of money from which he stole a few coins from time to time. Filimeno noticed him spending these coins at the store and hid his money some other place. Rocas Candelaria, who died at the age of 89 years in 1912 and who worked as a carpenter for Filimeno, claimed that Sanchez kept his money buried in two barrels.

Rocas noticed Eugenio twice a day looking in the fields for the money. When he finally found the barrels they were filled only with rags.

Apparently Filimeno never married but Santiago Padilla says his mother lived with him. Filimeno was one of the men who brought from Mexico the old bell of the church which is now in the present church. They baptized it Filimena, Manuela, Victoria y Dolores to commemorate the wives of the donors. Filimeno had an oratorio [private chapel] located in the nearby apple orchard for use of his family and employees. He preached the sermons and led the prayers. He was known as a person who could help injured people. Narciso Gomez, a local man, had gangrene or a cancer in one of his legs. He went to Filimeno for aid. Filimeno called the villagers together to obtain permission to amputate the leg. After receiving permission he cut off the leg with a butcher knife and cauterized the wound with hot tar. Narciso recovered.

It is reported that the patrones controlled nearly all the land and wealth in the village. They engaged intensively in the livestock business, having large herds of goats, sheep, cattle, and horses.

Economic System and Handicrafts

Agriculture was not as predominant a feature in the economy as it is today. Irrigation was practiced, utilizing water from the two dams. The methods were very primitive. A description of the plows is taken from the local newspaper, The Gringo and Greaser, February 15, 1884, Vol.I, No.1.

> "A Mexican plow is a curiosity worthy of place in an eastern
> museum. It consists of a crooked stick with an iron point nailed
> to it, or tied to it with a piece of rawhide, a small handle for
> the plowman to steer with and a pole to hitch the oxen to. This
> so-called plow will scratch a furrow in the soil about three
> inches deep, into which the seed is dropped and covered with the
> next round; it is now left to nature to rustle up a crop, for

nothing more is done except to reap. This is called farming in New
Mexico and strange as a general rule they gather in good crops.
The Mexican plow is the same the Egyptians used 5,000 years ago
and which the early Christians used thousands of years ago".

According to an informant, after the beans, the chief crop, came up
the farmers occasionally weeded the fields with a large iron-handled
hoe. Points of the plows and hoes were homemade.

The method of threshing beans was also primitive. The plants were
cut and piled on the ground, remaining there until dry. Then horses or
oxen were driven over the beans in a circular fashion until the beans
were separated from the pods. Then men with forks tossed everything into
the air, allowing the chaff to blow away while the heavier beans fell to
the ground.

In addition, other major crops were corn and chile, apples,
peaches and cherries. Native plants and game animals also were
important in local subsistence. Chokecherries were gathered and made
into preserves; gooseberries and cactus fruits were esteemed. Yucca was
used for soap and wild plants were used for greens and medicines. Deer,
antelope, rabbits and buffalo were major sources of protein.

Of all the natural resources eaten, buffalo meat was the most
important. During the Mexican period and well into the time of American
occupation the Spanish-Americans in the Rio Grande Valley and in
villages to the east buffalo hunting occurred in the fall. About
October, they started out in ox carts [carros de bueyes] for the plains
of west Texas. Several wagon owners banded together into groups of about
15 to 20 men. Wagon owners always took along several experienced buffalo
hunters [cazadores], hired on contract. The owners themselves rarely
hunted. For many days the parties traveled eastward until they arrived
at the plains in the vicinity of Lubbock, Texas, and the Red River
country (Hurt, 1941).

After sighting buffalo they would select a camp near a spring, lake or water course and have a meal prepared by the cocinero [cook]. Often there would be no wood near the camp but buffalo chips served for making fire. The next morning the hunter would ride out on fast trained horses that had lost their fear of the buffalo. When sighting a herd they would give chase. The animals were killed with a lance that had a steel point about a foot long. This point was hafted to a strong pole about five to six feet long. Only a few hunters had muzzle-loading rifles. The buffalo were stabbed at a point called the codillo below the shoulders. The hunters did not stop after stabbing the animals but continued in the chase until they had killed all the bison they wanted. In a single chase a hunter could bring down as many as 20 buffalo.

Each hunter was followed by a man called the seguidor on a slower horse whose job it was to kill the wounded buffalo with a dagger. Often this man would be riding many miles behind. Afterward the dead bison were thrown on to oxcarts and taken back to the camp. There they were skinned and most of the hides thrown away. The fat under the skin was taken off in large slabs and rendered into chicharones [cracklings]. The fat was also used for lard and for making manteca [butter]. The head, legs and hoof were not utilized, although the hip bones and ribs were sometimes taken back to Manzano to make caldo [soup]. Occasionally large bones would be split and the tritano [marrow] removed and then heated to make aceite [oil].

After the buffalo were skinned the meat was cut into slices and hung on a frame called una percha. This resembled a clothesline and consisted of a wood framework with rawhide lines. The strips of meat, called sesinas were allowed to dry overnight and the next day in the sun. The following day the meat was taken down, laid out on hides or grass and pounded to make jerky. Only cows were killed since the bulls were often too tough to eat. The tongues, considered a delicacy, were eaten during the time in camp.

At the end of the hunt the meat and bones were loaded into oxcarts and the party returned to Manzano. On arrival there was great rejoicing in Manzano. The families gathered around to meet and greet the hunters and afterwards there were many dances and parties. At Manzano the dried meat was sometimes ground in large stone mortars made of basalt. Manuel Griego has in his possession a large one that weighs about 300 lbs. It belonged to Antonio Padilla, his grandfather, who used to be a buffalo hunter.

On these long trips, the Manzaneños occasionally encountered Plains Indians, usually Apaches and Comanches. From them they learned many of their buffalo-hunting techniques. In the early period, nevertheless, they tried to avoid meeting the Indians while hunting as they were often at war with some of the tribes.

Clothing was often locally made for imported cloth was expensive due to the long and difficult supply route from Mexico. As a result it was customary for the men to wear the more easily made buckskin clothing and moccasins [tequas] while the women wore hand-woven garments. Sometimes flour sacks were modified for clothing. The moccasin tops were made from deer and buffalo and the soles of cowhide on which the hair was sometimes left. Awls for sewing hides were made from a sharpened L-shaped piece of deer antler. In winter for additional protection they wore skin leggings tied to their legs with the fiber from the yucca or palmilla and hide overshoes.

In preparing wool for weaving it was first washed, carded, and then spun on a wood spindle [travilla] similar to that used today by the

Navajos. This tool probably had a Mexican Indian origin for Parsons notes it among the Cora, Tarahumara and Zapotec but it also exists among the Pima and Pueblo Indians (1936:27). The tool itself consists of a shaft and a small whorl [malacate]. The spindle was turned by the fingers and not rolled on the thigh as the Navajo do. The cloth was woven on the large horizontal Spanish type of looms, never on the upright Navajo type of looms. Blankets were also woven by some of the mixed-blood people of Punta de Agua. They were of coarse wool with horizontal stripes. Barker describes the Spanish-American blankets as follows:

> "Designs on the old blankets are always simple. They were often only horizontal bands varying in color, width, and stitch. Yet each had as much individuality as the uniform pattern of our faces, and two were seldom alike." (1931: 253)

Examples of blankets made at Manzano are very rare and I have seen only two. One was made of plain brown wool and another had red and white stripes. Of the many blanket weavers in the area, best known was a Navajo woman, Guadalupe, who escaped confinement at Bosque Redondo and married Jesus Salas y Maria of Punta de Agua. According to Barker, the Spanish-American blankets were based upon a combination of Indian characteristics woven on a European loom (1931:253).

During the early years of the nineteenth century at Manzano locally made pottery was common although porcelain wares from Mexico were not present, judging by the sherd types found in the refuse heaps of the torreón and associated fortress buildings. Informants also state that metal cooking wares were present and obtained from traders. The local pottery was not only obtained from friendly Pueblo Indians but some of it was fabricated in Manzano and Chato, a small farming community a short distance to the south.

The pottery-making technique at Manzano, according to a local informant, was taught by a Navajo woman, Guadalupe Romero. The description of the technique is probably not accurate in all details. It is claimed that the women flattened a lump of clay tempered with sand into a tortilla shape and from this form shaped by hand the final vessel. Then it was scraped with a sharp stone or piece of gourd and let dry in the sun for three days. Afterwards the vessel was given a final polish by a stone and placed in a cow dung fire to be hardened. Usually the shapes were restricted to shallow bowls, large ollas and pitchers. Few small water ollas with handles were also represented. The pottery varied in color from black, orange, brown, to decorated jars of several colors. Plain black bowls were produced by coating the vessel with a thin layer of ground liver. Upon firing, this resulted in a carbonized black exterior. Black paint was made of a mixture of lard, ground white glass, and several other ingredients (a method which I question). Red paint was a mixture containing hematite. Designs, applied with a brush made of pig's hair, were not geometrical like Pueblo designs but consisted of such decorations as small flowers.

While the pottery-making technique was allegedly introduced to Manzano by a Navajo woman the description given above does not resemble in its the techniques, vessel surface, and vessel forms Navajo pottery (Hill 1937). In addition, no sherds encountered in the refuse heaps of the fortress, from the Penitente morada, or in the fill of the dam resemble Navajo pottery. In fact these sherds resemble closely the thick plain black and thick plain red sherds encountered in the ruins of the Quarai Mission and Convento, which may have been locally made, although ultimately having a Mexican origin.

The sherds I found at these locations in Manzano are characterized by being thick, poorly fired, sand tempered with a plain finish of black, gray, brick-red or cream colored. Only two sherds with designs were found: a simple red band on the rim with the remainder cream-colored. This description agrees more closely with information secured from another informant, a half-blood Indian, Jose Serna. He said that the pottery made at Manzano was of plain colors and rarely if ever had designs. At Chato an old man whose mother-in-law was a pottery maker stated that the coiled rather than the hand-modeled technique was used in the fabrication of ceramics.

Three whole jars were obtained at Manzano, all of which were reputed to be of local manufacture. One was a black pitcher that had a very greasy, dense black exterior that may owe its composition to the carbonized-liver technique described above. Another is a small reddish-brown jar that was excavated in the ruins of the first settlement of Manzano. The third is a small vessel with two handles. It is to be noted that all are thick, poorly fired, undecorated, and have a sherd temper.

The mano and metate were used for grinding meal for tortillas and still are occasionally used today, particularly for making nixtamal, a meal of blue corn. The local metate has three legs resembling those made in Mexico. Both the mano and the metate are made of basalt while those encountered in the nearby Pueblo Indian ruins are of sandstone or quartzite. Informants state that some of these grinding tools were locally made while others were obtained from a man at Tome who made them. Sometimes they were picked up from the nearby Pueblo ruins and put to use. The latter were not preferred, however, since being less hard particles of grit rubbed off when used and became mixed with the corn meal. In the early days in the houses, four manos and metates were

placed on a shelf-like bench [tepanco] built along one side of the main
room in the houses.

Four main types of house construction are present today in Manzano;
stone, adobe, jacal and log, and according to informants have always
been present (Figures, XII-XV). In the Land Grant Petition of 1829 it is
mentioned, "He shall construct a regular terraced house of adobe in the
plaza where the chapel is to be constructed." What is meant by terraced
house is not clear unless the houses of Manzano were to be built in the
terraced manner of the Pueblo Indian villages. At present the commonest
house type is the jacal, although it is not certain that this was the
main variety of the past. Carleton in 1846 mentions that the village was
built partly with logs set on end jacal fashion (1954) According to one
informant the oldest existing house at Manzano is the cement-plastered
structure opposite Tabet's general store.

The jacal house type (more commonly called casa de latas) at
Manzano was probably derived from the Indians of Mexico, although it is
also found among Southwest Indians, both in prehistoric and present-day
villages (Mindeleff 1896:237). This house was built by placing at the
corners four upright thick posts with forked tops. Then four posts were
laid on the form of a square or rectangle in the corners. A series of
smaller posts were placed vertically against the cross beams to form a
wall and the construction was completed by chinking and plastering the
walls. As is typical of Pueblo Indian houses the doorway is built too
low for a man of average height to enter without stooping. Vigas and
small cross sticks [latillas] are used in the roof structure. Over these
beams a layer of adobe is placed, although today gabled roofs made of
corrugated iron are common. House fronts are usually given a coat of

burned gypsum plaster [yeso]. On the house with flat roofs ashes were laid on top of the dirt covering to prevent leaking.

Furniture was all handmade and it was a common practice for the people to eat and sleep on the floor. Meals were cooked in hornos [fireplaces] ordinarily built in one corner of a room. Along the same wall at the opposite corner was a shelf of small poles plastered with mud. In the outside behind the houses were tepeistes, small structures of upright posts supporting a pole platform, upon which chiles, onions, and squashes were dried. In addition, meat, melons and squash were sometimes cut into strips and placed on outside lines to dry.

To light fires a device made of flint and steel [yecca] was used. This tool consisted of a U-shaped wire holding a piece of a flint. I observed one that had a long kerosene-soaked string or wick attached to a wire. In the last century, however, a long cord of lard-soaked oak bark also was used. The flint was struck with a piece of steel. Fire was extinguished by pulling a bone cylinder over the burning wick. I obtained one of these devices with a carved bone handle from Manzano.

The Manzaneños depended upon homemade candles and the glow of the fireplace for light; yet little light was needed since the people went to bed at sundown. Candles [velas] were made of the fat surrounding hog kidneys. The fat was cut into pieces and put in a pot over a fire. After melting it was poured over a frame from which strings were suspended. When the strings were coated with congealed drippings to the right length they were cut free and cooled. Thus a large number of candles were produced at once.

A common household utensil was the comal, a square pottery clay box with four stone legs. Informants claim that this artifact was made locally by potters. This was placed over a fire and used for cooking. Another type of <u>comal</u> was a flat stone slab used for cooking tortillas. Dippers were made of long gourds [<u>guajes</u>] in the manner of those of the Pueblo Indians. Food was measured with a type of balance scale, made of a small wood crossbar mounted on a wood post. To one end of the bar a stone shaped like a grooved maul was suspended by a leather thong; on the other end was a thong to which the material to be measured was tied. Much of the cooking was done outdoors in good weather in the typical Spanish-American dome-shaped adobe bake ovens [<u>hornos</u>].

Women carried water from the spring, Ojo del Gigante, in ollas balanced on their heads. In the village also there were several pit type of wells [<u>posos</u>]. One man, Pedro Marquez, built an elaborate water-raising device in an 85 foot well to the east of Manzano. It consisted of a series of buckets attached to a circular chain that ran on pulleys geared to a long bar at the top. This bar was pulled in a circular path by a team of oxen. By the spring east of Manzano there was a corn grinding mill. Here two large millstones were laid horizontally on the ground, one on top of the other. To the upper stone was attached horizontally a long pole which was pulled in a circular pattern by an ox team. According to informants this same technique was used in processing ore.

To prevent bears from robbing the fields and orchards to the north of the village, a large bear trap [<u>lovera</u>] was built. This consisted of a pit on top of which was placed a cross beam and to this beam a piece of horse meat was tied. Bears attempting to get the bait fell into the pit.

An instrument that was relatively rare at Manzano was the <u>vivuela</u>, a musical stringed bow, usually played by lonely shepherds. I obtained

an example made from a long bow-shaped sunflower stalk that had a tuning
peg at one end.   Tied to the other end and the peg was a single cat gut
string. The bow was placed in the mouth and the string was plucked, much
as a jaw's harp is played. Because this instrument has a   distribution
in many areas of the world its origin is unknown but probably in this
instance was Mexican in origin.

The tanning industry was primitive. One method was as follows: the
hide was taken from an animal, scraped and left to dry; it was then
dipped in cold water. The hair was removed by dipping in a mixture hot
water and bits of the wild gourd [calavazia]. The animal's brains were
then placed on the hide and it was folded raw side in,   then stretched
between two poles. After remaining thus in the sun for two days it was
taken down, beaten with a wood club until soft, greased again and
stretched once more in the sun for two days. It was then worked until
pliable and greased a third time. Another method of removing hair was to
bury it for about a week. In the use of brains for tanning the
Manzaneños shared a trait with Indians.

Syrup, a staple article, was made from locally-grown cane. After
the cane was cut and harvested, it was placed in a large barrel resting
over a fire. As the heat penetrated, the cane was mashed with a pole.
From the barrel the hot liquid flowed out through a tube into a large
wooden trough [canoa]. There the syrup was cooled and then poured into
large ollas. The women carried these jars home on top of their heads.
Some syrup was left in the canoa to harden, forming a candy called
melacocha.

The main vehicle for transportation was the oxcart, a homemade
article similar to those used today in rural regions of Mexico. These
carretas were lubricated occasionally with homemade brea [tar]. To make

this product a hole was dug in the ground and a fire was built in it.
Over the fire were placed green pine logs full of pitch. As the heat
drove the pitch from the logs men gathered it in buckets. It was then
mixed with lard for the finished product.

The Manzano method of lumbering was much different from that
practiced today in the Manzano Mountains. Selecting a tree, the
lumbermen climbed to the top and sawed down the middle, cutting branches
as they went along. When they had finished the tree fell into two large
already trimmed sections. Two men cut these sections into desired size
pieces with a large timber saw by one man standing in a pit under the
logs and another man standing over the pit. An alternate method was to
use a wood platform rather than a pit.

Religious Activities

The religious organizations at Manzano contributed greatly to the
solidarity of the community. In the village there were three religious
institutions: the Roman Catholic Church, the Penitentes, and the
services held in the private chapels of the patrones. Of the three, the
latter were the least important. The Catholic Church and the Penitentes
constantly vied with each other for priority.

The first mention of the Roman Catholic Church is in the Grant
Petition of 1824. It states: "He shall construct a regular terraced
house of adobe in the plaza where the chapel is to be constructed." Soon
after the year 1824, townspeople built the first church, a small,
square building surrounded by a circular wall, the latter feature for
protection against Indian raids. One informant stated that it was
located north of the torreón. Many years later another church was built,
a large cross-shaped building located on the site of the present church.

Best remembered of the early priests at Manzano was Padre Sembrano, a native of Mexico. Other pioneer priests, it is reported, were Padres Luis, Alejandro, Lamy, and Roberto.

The church wielded great influence over the every-day lives of Manzano as it did in other Spanish-American communities. It had control of birth, baptism, marriage, and death rites, and was a focus of religious activities, and sponsored many events such as fiestas of the annual patron saints' days, and Christmas and Easter ceremonies. The Roman Catholic Church did not conflict with the influence of the patrón over the peones but rather reinforced this system.

The Church and the patrones, nevertheless, did not have complete control of the religious and related activities of all the people of Manzano for they were forced to share power with the Penitente organization. Historical evidence suggests that the latter institution was a survival and outgrowth of the religious orders, confradias, (Dorothy Woodward, personal communication, November 19, 1939) that existed in Europe at the time of the Spanish Conquest. On the other hand, Henderson considers the Penitentes to be descended from the Third Order of St. Francis (1937:71). As with many other orders of the Roman Catholic Church during this period flagellation was widely practiced as a means of penance. According to Krodel,

> "From the 4th century self-inflicted flagellation was practiced by both the clergy and laity as the most efficacious form of penance...In the 16th century, Jesuits revived lay interest in self-inflicted flagellation, especially in the the southern European countries. Under their guidance the flagellant brotherhoods penetrated into Latin America." (1968:410-41)

This custom was carried by the Conquistadores into Mexico. The first record we have of flagellation in New Mexico was during the year 1598, when Don Juan de Oñate and his men performed public penance during Holy Week, under the guidance of the Franciscan Friars (Henderson

1937:71). Soon the institution known today as the Penitentes grew up in the Southwest. For the peón the Penitente brotherhood met the need for an emotional release from his servile position in which he was forced to work long hours, take orders from others, and repress his creative instinct. The Roman Catholic Church provided to a limited extent emotional expression but the fanatical character of the Penitente cult facilitated the release of pent-up emotions with abandon. While resembling in many details the Roman Catholic Church the Penitentes differed in that (1) its organization was open only to the members who underwent considerable physical suffering in the initiation rites, (2) most of its rites where held in secret and as such formed a common bond among the members and (3) physical suffering, that is flagellation, walking over cactus and rocks on bare knees and feet. In these respects the Penitentes resembled more closely some of the Pueblo Indian religious societies.

Penitente activities were centered in the morada [chapel] that lay on the hill top on the west side of Manzano. On the west side of the morada was a long room with a window to the west and a door to the east. The altar, surmounted by a large crucifix, was at the south end of the room while a small room on the east housed some of the paraphernalia, including whips [disciplinas]. These architectural features were confirmed by the ruins of the Manzano morada. In front of these ruins is a pile of stones supporting a large cross. It is reported that at one time this cross had 14 smaller crosses on its arms. Scattered about the ruins are many Spanish-American types of pot sherds. According to Bandelier, the morada was still being used when he visited Manzano in 1882 (Lange and Riley,1966:386). He describes the Manzano Penitentes cult in these words, "This abominable practice is very strong here and at Chilili."

Although the Penitentes had many different officers the only ones remembered are Jesús Saavedra, the hermano mayor [the leader of the organization] and Santiago Benevides, the pitero, the Penitente who played the pito [a small cane flute]. The father of the informant was a man who administered the cuts on the members' backs during the initiation ceremonies. The remaining officers were the rezador, who led the prayers and the cantador who led the songs.

The main ceremonies of the Penitentes were during Lent but they also met on other occasions such as the death of a member. On the first Wednesday of Lent (Ash Wednesday), the members gathered for the purpose of initiating new members and setting rules to be followed during the Easter season. Young boys desiring to join and who had reached the age of 15 were taken into the organization. From this day on the members moved into the morada where they lived for the duration of Lent. There the wives and mothers brought them food and other necessities. As they entered, they stripped in the antechamber, clothing themselves with only a breach clout to enter the main room, where they prayed, sang hymns, and fasted from time to time.

On Holy Thursday and Good Friday outdoor processions [processiones de sangre] were held. To call the people together the pitero blew his flute. As the members assembled, they took their place as follows: in the lead were members who were to flagellate themselves and a cross bearer, followed by the hermano mayor, the cantador, and the pitero, the latter playing a doleful melody. The other members came next. In the rear came the townspeople who were not Penitentes. Members were dressed in breach clouts and wore a black handkerchief over their heads to prevent recognition. As a means of penance the Penitentes lashed their shoulders with the _disciplinas_ until they bled. These whips were made of braided yucca cords with thorns, pieces of glass and nails tied to the ends. For additional penance they wrapped tight rawhide thongs about their legs and walked on their knees over the stony ground.

After several songs and prayers two companions lifted a heavy cross onto the back of the brother selected for the honored role of Christ in the reenactment of the crucifixion. The cross was so heavy that the bearer could only drag it along inch by inch, falling frequently and having to be lifted up by his companions. Slowly the procession moved from the _morada_ to the Calavario, a hill where the Calvary Cross stood. The brothers lashed themselves with wet whips, often dipping them in a bowl of the antiseptic, Romero tea. At the Calvary Cross the members knelt as the cross bearer dropped his burden and lay face downwards on the ground. After a short interval the companions again placed the cross on the bearer's back and the procession stumbled on to the cross that stood in the Manzano graveyard. Then the Penitentes walked back to the cross that stood in front of the chapel, sang and prayed and then entered the building. Thus, the procession ended.

During a year of drought the process ritual was varied by marching to the rim of El Cerrito, a hill about three miles east of Manzano. From there they looped southward and westward back to the _morada_, praying constantly for rain. At the start of the processions about 20 Penitentes participated but as they became exhausted more men took their place. Soon as many as 50 to 60 people were taking part.

On the whole, only men participated in the processions but according to one informant there were female Penitentes in Manzano before she was born. They had a small, single-roomed chapel furnished with a large table. In their processions, held at night, they carried no cross but only tortured themselves. Other informants state that in the procession given by the men women sometimes followed them.

During the last two days of Lent the Penitentes spent most of their time in the antechamber of the _morada_, some praying, others kneeling on gravel, the remainder lying on thorns and cactus, all of them fasting.

On Saturday before Easter, 15 men left the _morada_ and went to the Catholic Church, lying the entire day in the two doorways and asking the people to walk over them. In the evening in the _morada_ they held the _tenieblas_ ceremony, representing the darkening of the world after the crucifixion of Christ. Bull roarers, chains, and whistles gave an eery effect. Although it is not known whether at Manzano this was a ceremony for members only in the many rituals of this type that I have seen outsiders were permitted to be witnesses.

On Easter Day the Penitentes removed their masks for the first time. Then two men were tied with leather straps to the Calvary cross, hanging there until they fainted. As they grew weaker the _hermano mayor_ made a speech lasting about an hour. At the close of this ritual the Penitentes made their last return to the _morada_, while the _hermano mayor_ cut their backs as they stumbled along, causing them to bleed profusely and remove the last of their "poisoned blood". The cross bearer, exhausted by the long ceremonies, nearly always fainted en route and had to be carried to the chapel for treatment.

During the remainder of the year if a member died the Penitentes took the body from the chapel and moved it to the _morada_. They held a secret midnight procession to the graveyard, only Penitentes attending. Instead of placing the body in a coffin, it was dressed in white pants and a cross suspended from the neck. Afterwards the body was buried.

Santa Cruz Day (May 31) and Corpus Cristi Day were the other regular meeting times of the Manzano Penitentes. On the former day the morada was cleaned and refurbished; on Corpus Cristi Day, business matters were settled and the men who had committed crimes against other members were punished.

Manzaneños who were not members could ask the Penitentes to pray for them. For this service food was taken to one of the members who was praying in the morada during Holy Week. In addition, as the Penitentes marched around town in processions, they sometimes stopped at the houses to enter the private chapels, common at one time in Manzano.

The psychological effect of the Penitente order upon the people of Manzano should not be underestimated. While the Roman Catholic Church was a strong influence in shaping the character of some Spanish-Americans, the Penitente order was even stronger on others. The hardships and suffering required of the Penitentes drew them together in a band that in some aspects was stronger than family ties. For example, death ceremonies were performed in secret by only the members of the order. Furthermore, the hermano mayor literally had the power of life or death over the Penitentes. A prospective member was obliged to swear to abide by the organization rules, even excluding his family from the secrets. The high religious tension during Lent left them so exhausted, physically and mentally, that it was only once during the year that they could afford the satisfaction of this release from their monotonous existence. In addition to providing religious and emotional outlet for the members, the Penitente order had an influence on the judicial structure of the community. According to Austin, matters which otherwise might have been brought to the civil courts were settled by the local hermano mayor due to the fact that civil courts were either too distant

or unsympathetic to the people's needs (1924:372). In addition, the
infermo, a Penitente official, was often appealed to by the peones for
health and other medical advice (1924:372)

Family Organization

A major integrating feature of Manzano society was a highly
organized family structure. It was also the institution which provided
many services now offered today by institutions outside the home.

Education , for example, took place largely in the home for there
were no public schools in Manzano during the period when it was part of
Mexican territory. This meager education was supplemented by the small
amount of learning that took place prior to catechism classes in the
Roman Catholic Church. Choice of marriage partners rested largely in the
hands of the parents. Much informal recreation centered in the home. In
the evenings when families joined together many Spanish-American and
Indian games were played. Visits between the families tended to unite
the village members. Children had great respect for their parents,
usually obeying the latter's wishes without question, according to
local informants.

Summary and Conclusions

During the period when Manzano was part of the Territory of Mexico
there were many institutions and customs that integrated the village
into a tight social-cultural unit. These include the Roman Catholic
Church, the Penitente order, the peon-patrón system, the communal
buffalo hunts, the right of the community to labor for such activities
as maintaining the reservoirs and irrigation ditches, the Land Grant

Commissioners, the organization of the community for defense against Indian raids, the custom of capturing Indians for slavery and the Water Commissioners.

Indian cultural traits were adopted whenever they promised to aid the community in adjusting to the harsh environment. The Indian items borrowed were mainly techniques of manufacturing material objects such as blankets, house construction, food preparation, and bows and arrows, spears, pottery, and the custom of carrying water on the head in _ollas_ [water jars]. On the other hand, borrowing of non-material traits were rare. Examples of the latter type included the presence of many Indian words in the vocabulary, the practice of scalp taking, the scalp dance and various kinds of games. Furthermore, only a few of these traits were borrowed from the Indians of New Mexico, for historical evidence indicates that most of them were incorporated into Spanish-American culture from Mexican Indians. For example, the words of Indian derivation listed in the Appendix XII have an Aztec derivation rather than a Navajo, Apache or Pueblo Indian origin. These include such words as _metate_ [a grinding stone], _jacal_ [a house type], _tepalcate_ [pot sherd], _tepocate_ [tadpole] and _guajalote_ [buzzard].

CHAPTER IV

MANZANO DURING THE EARLY AMERICAN PERIOD

On August 15, 1846, New Mexico was taken by General Stephen W. Kearny and in 1848 by the Treaty of Guadalupe Hidalgo became a territory of the United States. With the entrance of Lieutenant Abert and a small force at Manzano, November 3, 1846, a new period of acculturation began in the village, that of Anglo-American acculturation. From Abert's account comes this interesting description,

> "We caught sight of Manzano when but midway between it and our morning's camp. It is one of the largest towns that we have met with on the west side of the river. Many of their houses have their fronts neatly whitewashed, and the church has its whole facade whitewashed with a preparation of calcined selenite. This mineral is often used as a substitute for window sashes.
>
> "When we first neared the town, several of the inhabitants came out to meet us with guns in their hands. The people still have a lingering inclination for the old government, and although none of their institutions have changed, yet, it will be some time before they will regard the entrance of Americans as otherwise than an intrusion. We camped near the acequia that feeds the mills of the town, after passing through most of the central streets of the place. Near our camp, there was a large grove of apple trees; and on the east side [west] of the town, near the mountains, a second grove. The trees were planted very close together.
>
> "In the afternoon, we visited the town and its environs. On the west toward the mountains, there is a large dam, constructed of crib work. Twelve feet wide and eight feet high, and a hundred feet long, formed of rough logs, and the interior is filled with stones and earth. Just now the lake is nearly dried up, and the little mills that its water used to turn have not sufficient power to grind the millers' corn. (Walter 1916: 19).

The next historical record of Manzano is found in the official correspondence of James B. Calhoun (1850: 281). He states,

54

"The Jicarillas Apaches, remain yet in the neighborhood of Manzano. (See my letter No. 86 Nov. 5, 1850.) They visit Manzano whenever they choose, and buy and sell without hindrance. Their chief capital is known to be so, so I am informed by Dr. Connolly, the mules which they stole from him and other, of which I advised you by my letter No 76, August 30,1850."

Calhoun states in his correspondence of March 31, 1851:

"The Navajos continue in small parties, to commit depredations, and have not the slightest idea that we can effectually check them. They never regard the loss of a few men and captives. A few days since, the Navajos drove off stock from near Manzano. The Apaches, whose localities have been in that neighborhood for months past, ascertained the fact, pursued the Navajos, recovered and returned the stock and brought in a scalp. Four were wounded and three have died since...

"Lieut J. P. Holliday, 2d Dragoons, left Albuquerque on the 18th with forty men in search of Indians who had committed depredations in the neighborhood of Manzano. He found the camp of the Apaches, sixty miles E. or S. E. of Manzano... The Superior Chief of the Apaches East of Del Norte, Chacon, approached Lieut Holliday, and inquired the object of his visit; declaring that his people had committed no depredations of a recent date, and at once agreed to return with the Lieutenant, and he and others are expected here on the 3rd of the ensuing month." (Abel 1915:307-308)

From Calhoun's account it is evident that during the early period of American contact the Apache continued to be friends and the Navajos enemies of the Manzaneños. They were also friendly with some of the other Plains Indians. According to Lucas Zamora an elderly informant, the buffalo hunters of Manzano had friendly intercourse with the Comanche Indians, often learning to speak the language. Calhoun's observations that the Navajos were enemies is borne out by a tale told in Manzano of the massacre of a local miner by this tribe of Indians.

In 1855, Major James Carleton led a military excursion into Manzano. His diary gives the following description of the village,

"The town of Manzano is situated at the base of the sierra of that name, and a small rivulet, which running eastward to the open plains, soon sinks into the ground. Several dams are constructed along this rivulet to collect and retain the water for purposes of irrigation. The town is built partly on logs set on end jacal fashion, with the interstices filled with mortar, and the roof covered with earth, and partly with adobes. It sports a very dilapidated church, erected it would seem, as a practical antithesis to the morals of the inhabitants; for Manzano enjoys pre-eminently the wide-spread notoriety of being the resort of more murderers, robbers, common thieves, scoundrels, and vile abandoned women than can be found in any town of the same size in New Mexico. Fortunately it contains but few inhabitants, not more than five or six hundred at the most. It is not an old town. When the settlers came here they found two groves of apple trees, one just above the site occupied by the town and one just below. Tradition says that these trees were planted at the time Manzano and Quarra [Quarai] were inhabited, and yet, tradition has lost all trace of when that time was. It is said that the Catholic Church of New Mexico claims that they were planted by some priest, but admits that it has no records of authentic traditions about the ruins we have visited. Her claim, however, that some priest did this at some period or the other is good enough to authorize her to farm out these two orchards yearly, as we were informed to the highest bidder. Two of the largest trees in the lower grove were found to be respectively eight and six feet in diameter. The largest was hollow -- a mere shell of an inch or two in thickness. These trees have a venerable appearance. They never have been pruned, and therefore have grown gnarled and scraggly. Many are much smaller than the ones we measured. They have grown, doubtlessly, from seeds which have fallen from the older ones. How long this process of self-planting has been kept up, of course, no one can know. Apple trees are not indigenous to New Mexico. Assuming this to be true, however, that the largest of these trees were planted at the period referred to, then the ruins of Abo and Quarai are more than two centuries old.

"There are two groves, or rather two clumps of these trees, are not standing regularly in rows or orchard-like; on the contrary, they are crowded together in the most irregular and natural manner.

"The name of the town, and of the towering sierra to the west of it, was adopted from finding these orchards here, Manzana being the Spanish for apple, and Manzano being the botanical name in that language for apple tree. The name of the town is spelt indiscriminately in both ways through out New Mexico.

"Immediately about Manzano, and up the slope towards the high mountains west of the town, there is a fine forest many miles in extent, of most excellent timber for boards and for building purposes. Some twenty-five or thirty miles in an easterly direction there is a large salt lake which has no outlet. This lake supplies nearly the whole of the upper portion of the territory with salt. There are fine roads leading toward it from different directions.

"We had procured orders from the vicar general of New Mexico for what corn we should require at Manzano--corn which had been paid in by the peasants as tithes (diezmos) to the Catholic Church. When we arrived there we found that the corn belonging to the church was some six or seven miles off at another village, called Torreon. So we were forced to buy on credit what forage we required.

"An American named Fry, a hunter, who lives at Manzano, went out to see the ruins with two Mexicans to meet these Texans...After traveling six miles, we struck an Indian trail which leads from Manzano to the country of the Mescalero Apaches." (1854-304)

In another portion of Carleton's diary he remarks,

"From what we have observed during our second visit to the place, this Botany Bay of New Mexico, we have concluded that our former estimate of the character of the inhabitants was premature and ill-judged, we now believe that there is not one single redeeming trait of disposition or habits to be found within the border." (1854:315-316)

Although Carleton's opinion of the character of the people of Manzano may be the result of the fact that these people still had not fully accepted the Americans as other than intruders there is, however, evidence that his statements had some basis in fact. For example, I found at Tomé a folk poem stating that the people of Manzano robbed Spanish-Americans that entered their village.

Adolph F. Bandelier, the well known Southwestern historian and traveler, visited Manzano several times in 1882 and 1883 but his Journals contain little information on this village. In his visit with Padre Louis Bourdier on December 25 he states that the priest

"...received us with open arms and insisted upon our staying here, at the Curacy. He complains bitterly of his people, says that they are extremely ignorant and brutish ...There is no irrigation here; the crops depend upon rain for their growth." (Lange and Riley, 1966:386)

He also states that there were four pueblos at Manzano, one on the hill of the Penitentes, one on the south side of the creek near the Aboleda, one opposite the Loma, and one at Ojitos (Lange and Riley, 1966:387).

It is quite possible that the pueblo near Ojitos is the original site of Manzano itself. Both the first and second sites he mentions above have Pueblo Indian types of pot sherds on their surface. His statement, however, that there was no irrigation at Manzano is not supported by earlier and later accounts of visitors to the village.

On January 2, 1883 Bandelier again visited Punta de Agua and Manzano. He states that a man shot himself at the maquina [saw mill ?] of Eusebio Garcia, so the Padre had to go there to administer. The location of the mill is uncertain. At Punta de Agua Bandelier states that, "I was told here that the people at Abó had been frightened of my [arrival], somebody at Manzano having told them that I came with the intention of taking away their land and houses." (Lange and Riley 1970:11-12)

After New Mexico became a territory of the United States the Anglo-Americans rarely moved into this village as residents. As mentioned above the hunter named Fry was seen in the town by Major Carleton in 1855. A local informant states that a man named Johnson, who operated a refinery near the salt lakes, lived for a time at Manzano. The first record of a large number of American settlers moving into the Estancia Valley was that of a group of people from Oklahoma who founded the village of Eastview, a few miles south of Manzano, in 1861. It is reported that they were a band of outlaws driven from their state and seeking refuge. Apparently their community did not last long due to the hostilities of the Manzaneños; soon they were forced to move.

One of the prominent Americans residing at Manzano was Charles L. Kusz. According to Green, Kusz is listed as postmaster with the office of postmaster having been established February 28, 1881 (1882:181). It also listed "Kusz & Co., Assayers, Surveyors, etc. According to Lange and Riley, Kusz was the Commissioner of Valencia County in 1884 (1970:356). Polk and Danser listed Kusz as postmaster, livestock breeder, real estate dealer and proprietor of the newspaper the Gringo

and Greaser (1884:337). This newspaper was published semimonthly during
the years 1883 - 1884. According to Anderson,

> "The assassination of Charles L. Kusz, Jr. editor of the Gringo
> and Greaser at Manzano, Valencia County on March 26, 1884, caused
> high feelings throughout New Mexico. The editor was killed while
> seated at the table at his home by two rifle shots fired through
> the window. He was entertaining Dr. John M. Bradford at dinner,
> and they were alone. His paper was an authority on mining and
> ranching in New Mexico and the only paper in the world printed
> entirely in italics. It is believed that the assassination was due
> to his fearlessness in discussing public affairs, especially on
> account of his efforts to expose cattle thieves." (1907 I:241-242)

A local source stated that Kusz's home was near the dam.

In an advertisement in the Gringo and Greaser reference is made to
a Mr. Guzman, an engineer who sold locally mining supplies. The lumber
industry after 1885 attracted several Anglo-Americans and Spanish-
Americans from other communities to Manzano. It is reported that a man
named Eugenio Romero, a politician and prominent man from Las Vegas, was
the first to invest in the Manzano lumber business; while a Mr. Dunn and
Mr. Spencer were the first Anglo-Americans to become interested. They
operated a small saw mill that was moved from canyon to canyon in the
Manzano Mountains as the supply of timber ran out in each location.
An advertisement in the Gringo and Greaser makes reference to a Mr.
Sigals, who was a silversmith and blacksmith, making rings, bracelets,
spurs, bridle bits and knives. His father brought the mail from
Chihuahua City to Santa Fe and then to Manzano and back in an eight mule
team stage coach.

The Influence of American Culture on Manzano in the 19th Century to 1910

Acculturation with the Anglo-Americans was far more pervasive for
the Manzaneños than that with the American Indians, for now they had the
status of conquered people in contrast to their earlier position as

conquerors. As mentioned previously, the Spanish-Americans had the freedom to pick and choose those elements from Indian culture which they considered as adding to their chances for survival. No longer was this choice available to them, although this did not prevent their trying to resist many traits of American culture.

After Manzano became American territory the traditional social economic institution known as the peon-patrón system soon felt the effects of the bill of March 2, 1867, of the United States which formally abolished peonage or debt servitude (Woodson 1968). Thus at Manzano the first egalitarian, democratic social order evolved involuntarily.

Nevertheless, a form of peonage still prevailed in the partido system which was protected as late as 1923 by a law of the State of New Mexico which recognizes the validity of owner's contracts. In this system a sheepherder borrows a certain number of sheep, usually about 100 ewes, from an owner and by contract agrees to return a certain number of sheep by an agreed-upon date, generally about 20 lambs at the end of a year. In addition, the renter had to rent rams from the owner and sell his sheep and wool through the owner's store. In return the renter usually had rights to graze the sheep on the owner's land. The main problem arises when the borrowed sheep because of one misfortune or other did not reproduce sufficiently to pay this amount. According to a report of the United States Forest Service, one of the methods by which the sheepherders are induced to enter a contract is to work out debts that are owed to the owner's store (United States Department of Agriculture 1940). According to Charles, "By such unethical methods and by encouraging the renter to incur heavy indebtedness, the patron was about to foreclose on the property put up as security for the fulfillment of the contract." (1940:56) Although the partido system was common in New Mexico in the last quarter of the past century I have no data on how common this institution was at Manzano.

Other than the obvious freeing of the Indian slaves at Manzano with the laws abolishing slavery and peonage the additional effects of these laws upon institutions at Manzano is controversial. One local informant stated that this action incensed the patrones and they demanded that the peones who asked to be free of their obligations give back everything they had earned before they could become free agents. There is reason to believe that not all if any patrones at Manzano fell into this category. According to several other informants, at least the peones of Filimeno Sanchez had a high regard for his kindly nature. Informants also state that although the abolition laws freed the slaves and peones not many people in this case took advantage of their new rights and sought other employment. In this characteristic the slaves and peones at Manzazno resembled the actions of many Black slaves after the Civil War.

After Manzano became an American Territory there was for a long time little change in the economy other than the dissolution of the peon-patrón system. Livestock raising, mainly of sheep, continued to be the chief source of income supplemented by agriculture and trading. Not until the 1880s did lumber become an important industry. It was, however, a source for employment since the owners were outsiders. Mining apparently was never very important mainly because of the scarcity of local mineral resources. The traditional arts and crafts persisted since Manzano was relatively isolated from the Anglo-American markets in the cities of the Rio Grande Valley of goods that came along the Santa Fe Trail. Each home had an altar with carved wooden statues and painted tablets of the saints.   The blacksmiths did a lively trade and   one of

the best known was the above mentioned Mr. Sigals.

Traditional agriculture practices continued during the early Anglo-

American period. Lieutenant Abert gives the following description of the

flour mills at Manzano:

> "These mills, like everything else in New Mexico, are of a very
> primitive style. There is a vertical axis, on the lower end of
> which is a water wheel;   the other end passes through the lower
> burr, and is firmly connected with the upper stone,, which, as
> the axis turns, revolves around the lower stone. Above all this,
> hangs a large hopper of ox-hide, kept open at the top by a square
> frame, and narrowed off toward the bottom, so as to present the
> form of an inverted cone. In the extremity of the bag is a small
> opening, and this is fastened to a little trough. One end of this
> trough being supported at its connection with the hopper, the
> other end, or mouth, is sustained by a horizontal strip of wood,
> of which an extremity rests on the upright, and the other is
> upheld by an inclined burr, so that the motion to the trough and
> hopper-------?; thus the grain falls into the opening in the burr,
> and passes out between the two burrs." (Walter 1919:21)

Prior to the settlement of the Estancia Valley by the Anglo-

Americans this region was part of the vast open ranges of eastern New

Mexico. According to local informants in the past century thousands of

cattle wintered near the salt lakes, returning to the juniper and pinyon

cedar-clad foothills in the summer. Before the county became overgrazed

the grasslands were in good condition with the grass in some places

being waist high to a horse. It was during this period that Manzano

reached its peak of prosperity. As the grazing land was taken over by

homesteading Anglo-American farmers after 1905 the livestock gradually

became secondary in importance. It is noteworthy, however, that during

the next 15 years the number of cattle increased despite the shrinking

of grazing land. Since then, the number and value of cattle has

declined (United States Department of Agriculture 1940:312). The same

trends characterize the raising of sheep, which at one time were more

important in the economy than the raising of cattle.

During the last century mining in the Manzano Mountains also was of some importance in the Manzano economy. In Lieutenant Abert's diary reference was made to mining as follows:

> "While there, I made the acquaintance of 'El Senor Don Pedro Baca, one who has charge of the silver mines. He told me that there are, in the mountains, mines of silver, copper, iron and azogue; by this last word, I understand him to mean quicksilver, but in the strict mining language, azogue is used to mean silver ore adapted for amalgamation; for the ores that I brought to the United States, and which he called azogue, do not contain any mercury." (Walter 1916:21)

Another indication of the mining industry at Manzano is an advertisement in the Gringo and Greaser which states "Goodman and Zeiger, Manzano, New Mexico, Miners and Ranchers supplies". One informant said that Goodman was an engineer for a mill started by Eusebio Garcia in 1881. Although not certain the mill was probably used for processing ore.

Folktales abound in Manzano about mines. One concerns Juan Soldado who had a mine near Capillo Peak in the Manzano Mountains. Informants disagree as to whether he was an Indian or Spanish-American. It is said that one time when he was coming from his mine to Manzano with 14 mules loaded with gold a band of Indians intercepted him. Juan pushed the animals over a cliff in a deep canyon, killing them immediately. No one is sure if the Indians killed Juan. Some say he was killed as a soldier in the war between Mexico and the United States. After his death many Manzaneños attempted to find the mine. While herding sheep José Zamora, the uncle of Lucas Zamora, a living informant, and several other men found the mine in 1862. The men entered the mine and saw a vein with gold and found a bag containing chisels and other digging tools. José, being a very religious man who deplored the bad influence of gold on men, swore to God that no one else would find the mine. He then covered up the entrance with wood and dirt. For years Manzaneños tried to find the mine without success. One day a sheepherder from Tomé, an employee of a man named Otero, came to Manzano and on the way accidentally found the mine. He then hurried back to the mountains to tell another sheepherder of his discovery. Unfortunately, they never could find the mine.

During the early period of American occupation until about 1877 buffalo hunting furnished a major means of subsistence at Manzano. In this period firearms became widely used as were American-made wagons such as the Murphy wagon that took eight oxen to pull it. It was five feet high, five feet wide and fourteen feet long and could hold, according to informants, the buthered meat of about 120 bison, a total weight of about 700 lbs. If these figures were true, which there is reason to doubt, they indicate that only the tongue and hump meat were saved. Another wagon was the "army type" that had iron axles and took six oxen to pull it. It could hold the meat of about 90 buffalo.

The length of the hunt varied, depending upon the distance traveled, success of the kill and the weather. Sometimes the hunt took two months, lasting into the winter. In the part of the Texas panhandle where they hunted they usually did not run into too much snow or blizzards. Surplus meat brought to Manzano was generally sold in Albuquerque, Sante Fe or Las Vegas for about 25 cents a pound.

After 1876 bison became too scarce for the people from Manzano to hunt. One informant stated that the Texans killed the last bison on the Staked Plains with guns.

Julian Sanchez of Manzano tells this story of his only hunt. He left the village on October 3, 1876 with a party of local hunters and men from Lincoln, New Mexico. Only two wagons were used. At that time he was only 17 years old and was assigned duty as cook's helper since he was considered too young and inexperienced to be a hunter. After traveling about 300 miles they reached the Staked Plains and camped near a large salt pan called the Ojo de Aguilas. Sanchez and a young inexperienced hunter named Jaramillo saw an old bison. Sanchez aimed his rifle at the bison but since he did not know what spot to aim at the animal, held his fire. He was also afraid to shoot since he was in open country with no place to find refuge from a wounded bison. His uncle from Belen had better luck since he dug himself in a pit by a water hole and was able to kill several animals. The last buffalo that Sanchez saw was an old bull on the Staked Plains east of Pinos Wells.

Another hunter, Francisco Aragon, who was born in Chato on December 3, 1866, went on his first buffalo hunt when he was seven years old with his father. They traveled in large ox carts with canvas tops that were pulled by eight bison. They camped on the Staked Plains near Lubbock, Texas. At that time the grass was very high. On this trip there were only four hunters and they killed between 70 to 80 bison. They hunted on horse with five-foot lances and firearms. They left the bones and hides. At this time they wore leather clothes. They never had any trouble with the Plains Indians that they met. His father was afraid of these Indians and always avoided them when possible.

As Aragon became older he earned his living driving ox carts, pulled by eight animals, hauling supplies between Las Vegas and Lincoln and traveling along the Pecos River. One of his favorite watering places was Pinos Wells near Carrizozo. Judging by a local song cowboys from Manzano participated in cattle drives in Kansas and throughout the Southwest. These cattle drives were also a subject of a ballad called Campana that describes the nostalgia of the cowboys when they were away from Manzano.

Amicable relations continued with the Apache Indians. According to Timio Luna a large band of Apache under the famous chief Manuelito approached Punta de Agua by the acequia on the east side of the village. They fightened the local people and the women and children fled to the fortress in Manzano. Seeing this flight the Apache Indians displayed a large white banner, indicating the peaceful nature of their visit. The women and children came out of the fortress and everyone conversed. Manuelito and his band went on their way. A few days later they raided near Santa Fe. On their return trip to the Gallinas Mountains Manuelito was killed by American soldiers under the command of Kit Carson (Twitchell 1912:325). To commemorate this event the people of Manzano used to sing a song written by Sancho Chavez of Torreón called the Indita de Manuelito [Ballad of Manuelito] (Appendix IV). Older informants at Manzano still remember the Indita de Victorio [Ballad of Victorio] said to be written by Mecias Coyasos of Los Lunas about Victorio the chief of the Ojo Caliente Apaches who was killed by Mexican troops in 1880 (Hodge 1907: 64).

Stories regarding the problems with the Navajos was also a subject for ballads sung at Manzano. Below is the only part of a ballad still remembered that was written by José Luis Lovato about the capture of his wife by the Navajos,

José Luis andando en Mora   José Luis was going to Mora
Cuando el caso sucedió: When the following thing happened:
Se llevan a su familia   They carry off his family
Para centro del Navajo.   To the center of the Navajo.

En el camino donde iban   On the road where they traveled
Tiran una taza y un plato   They throw a glass and a plate
Para ver si las seguia   To see if he would follow them
Señor José Luis Lovato.   José Luis Lovato.

Manuel Griego remembers a song written about Nana Lupe who was captured by the Navajos. While a captive judging by the words of the song below her Navajo husband sold her services to other Indians.

Buenas tardes le de Dios.	Good morning to you.
¿Como esta Usted cunado?	How are you brother-in-law?
¿Quiere Usted que el durmiendo	Do you wish him sleeping
Esta noche conmigo?	This night with me?
Quitate de aquel indio	Get rid of that indian
¿Y donde es el dinero que	And where is the money
De traes tu?	That you bring?
Arrimate pa'ca y contaremos	Come over here and we will count
El dinero ¿ y pa'que quieres	The money and why do you want
Tu el contado el dinero	Him counting the money while
Que yo dando?	I am putting out?

Chorus:

Ene gellana gellana yo	Ene gellana gellana yo
Ene gellana gellana yo.	Ene gellana gellana yo.

Troubles continued with the Navajos until their conquest by Kit Carson and their removal to the Bosque Redondo near Fort Sumner. A well-remembered story concerns the death of Juan José Turrieta, the father of Florentino (Appendix XV) and the great uncle of Lucas Zamora's wife (Appendix XIII). To escape the Civil War draft the father took his son into the Manzano Mountains. He also had with him a dog and a herd of goats. After several days he sent Florentino to Manzano for groceries. That night the dog came into the village with an arrow in his back. Everyone knew immediately that something serious had happened to the elder Turrieta and a large group of men went to the camp. There they found Turrieta was dead and filled with arrows. Near him was a pair of buckskin moccasins with cow hide soles that he was making when he was killed. Suddenly the Manzaneños spied a band of about 60 Navajos. Both sides let loose a volley of bullets and arrows. At that time most of the men from Manzano were armed with bows and arrows. After the initial exchange of fire the Indians fled further into the mountains and in time the Manzaneños gave up the chase. He was killed above the present CCC camp in Red Canyon. In honor of Turrieta a canyon in the Manzano Mountains where he was killed was named after him.

Enecleto Pena, a local man, had two scars on his knee from a fight with a Navajo. One time when he was riding horseback he ran onto this Indian also on a horse. Enecleto grabbed the Indian by his chongo [pig tail] and they both fell to the ground. Then Enecleto grabbed a knife from his belt and tried to stab the Navajo. Just then another Indian rode up and shot Enecleto twice in the knee with arrows. Fortunately a local man rode up and shot this Indian. The other Navajo then fled. Enecleto was a large man with a full beard who was at one time the schoolmaster at Punta de Agua.

Other stories also indicate the danger from the Navajos in trips outside of Manzano. Juan Cisneros was traveling through the Sierra Oscura Mountains when he was ambushed by an Indian. He was able to grab the Indian by his pig tail. Throwing the man to the ground he cracked his skull and soon the Indian died.

Ciprian Torres, when a boy, left La Cienega, a farming settlement near Manzano, in an ox cart going to Lincoln, New Mexico. One night the party camped about five hundred yards from a spring and Ciprian was sent on a mule to the spring to bring back a barrel of water. As he neared the spring the saw a Navajo lying on his stomach drinking water from a gourd. Cipian lifted his rifle and shot the Indian. Suddenly 14 Navajos, who were sleeping nearby, jumped up. He began to scream and shout for help. This frightened the Indians and they fled.

Once a large band of Indians stole many herds of livestock from the Estancia and Rio Grande Valleys. To recover the animals a band of Spanish-Americans under the command of Blas Lucero took out after them.

After riding for several days they encountered the Navajo in the Sierra Oscura Mountains. When the Indians saw their pursuers they ran to the other side of a canyon and disappeared. It was a dangerous place to follow the Indians for one misstep would cause the Manzaneños to fall off a cliff. For the first time Lucero, a very brave man, was afraid to go on even though they could see the stolen livestock further down the canyon near the Indian camp. Finally Jose Archuleta, a brother of Juan Archuleta the commander of the vigilantes at Torreón, urged the party to go on, telling them they could only die once. He was younger and, therefore, less cautious than Lucero. Eleven of some 50 men stayed behind with Lucero and the others followed Archuleta.

As Archuleta's party went along the west rim of the canyon and descended into the Navajo's camp the Indians went around the east rim. As a result the two groups came in sight of each other. The Navajos began to flee again but their chief told them to halt. The chief then signaled to the Spanish-Americans that he wanted to talk. As he stepped forward, Johnson, an Anglo-American living at Manzano, also walked forward and shot the Indian chief. Fighting broke out immediately. After a long time the only Navajo left alive was a young man. He approached the Spanish-Americans cowering and saying "Tata, Tata". The Indian had shot his bow so much that his wrist was cut open, exposing his sinews. On the return trip he had to sleep between Archuleta and Johnson. During his time as a captive in Manzano, the Navajo incurred the hatred of Manuel Torres of Punta de Agua. Torres wanted to kill the Indian but was not allowed this action. After several fights between the Navajo and Torres the Indian challenged the latter to a duel with guns. The Manzaneños then gave them permission to so settle their enmity. The Indian and Torres rode off to a canyon near Abó, each armed with a gun.

Torres became scared, whirled around and shot the Indian. For his
cowardly trick Manuel was named El Beyota [knot head]. When the stolen
livestock were returned to Manzano their owners came from a wide area to
reclaim them.

Not all Navajós who lived at Manzano and in the nearby settlements
were brought there as captives. For example Guadalupe, the well known
blanket maker, escaped from the confinement of her people at the Bosque
Redondo in 1880 and moving to Punta de Agua married a local man.

During the last century the Penitente organization continued to be
strong. According to Austin it became influential in politics throughout
New Mexico during the early period of American influence (1924:371).
This occurred in two ways: either the leader, the hermano mayor, was
already the local political chief, or local politicians when first
elected were inducted into the Penitente order. For example, at the town
of San Mateo, New Mexico, the Penitentes made an honorary member a local
Anglo-American sheep owner who lived nearby. The Penitentes' strength in
local state politics is shown by its becoming incorporated under the
laws of the State of New Mexico as provided for by all such fraternal
types of organization (Austin 1924:355).

As a result of open competition between the Penitentes and the
Roman Catholic Church for control over the lives of the Spanish
Americans Bishop Salpointe in 1899 placed a ban on the Penitentes. A.
Espinosa gives a different interpretation, however, on the order given
by the Bishop to disband the Penitentes (1911:636). He attributes the
Bishop's order to the Penitentes having carried their fanaticism to an
undesirable extreme. According to local informants Padre Sembrano,
resident priest at Manzano, forced the disbandment of the Penitentes at
Manzano in the last of the 1880s. As previously mentioned their chapel

was still being used during the visit of Bandelier in 1882. Padre Guatier, the present priest at Manzano, sold the images of the saints and other religious objects of the Penitentes to collectors. Thus, the power of the Penitentes was broken at Manzano although it has continued to exist in many New Mexican villages such as at Chilili.

With the abandonment of the Penitente order at Manzano its functions were transferred to the local Roman Catholic Church. The influence of the Church had always been strong at Manzano but now it was much stronger. It is doubtful, however, if the intense feeling of brotherhood among the Penitentes was transferred to the Roman Catholic Church, with the end result that social solidarity at Manzano was weakened.

At an unknown date the original church at Manzano was razed and a new church with a cruciform shape was built on the site of the present church. It is reported to have had walls 50 feet high but this is probably an exaggeration. The present church (Figure VI) and convento (Figure VII) were built before 1876, according to local informants. Archbishop Lamy presided over a wide district that included Manzano and the town of Lincoln to the south in the White Mountains. His nephew, Father Antonio Lamy, was sent to Lincoln to pray for the soul of a man about to be hanged. Kneeling there in the shadow of the scaffold and seeing the tragedy of human life he became deeply depressed. Padre Lamy returned sorrowfully to Manzano and soon fell sick. In a short time he died of grief in a room in the convento. He was buried in front of the main altar in the present church on his 28th birthday, according to a carved stone block in front of the altar brought there by his father. The present priest, Father Guatier, assumed his charge in 1895.

The Roman Catholic Church at Manzano has continued until present to exercise control over the life of the people of Manzano. Their religious, emotional and family life was under direction of the Church. Through fiestas and other religious holidays the Church provided an important recreational function. What little formal education the people had during the last century came through sermons, catechism classes and personal talks by the priests. A major complaint of many Manzaneños is what they consider to be excessively high fees for such services as weddings and christenings.

Life with the Manzaneños was not entirely a matter of labor and religion; recreational activities of a secular nature occupied much of their time. A common sport of the past was known as the "corrido de gallo", usually played on San Juan's Day, June 24th. In this game, a chicken or similar object was buried in the sand with only one part projecting. A group of horsemen formed behind a line took turns trying to pull the object from the sand. If any man was successful he had to carry it beyond a line and escape the other players who pursued him. According to informants, in about the year 1898 Antonio Sanchez y Pacheco was killed near the Manzano spring while participating in this sport. As a result the game was abandoned, although it is still played in the neighboring town of Torreón.

Dancing was one of the most common forms of entertainment. Lieutenant Abert who visited Manzano November 3, 1846, describes a local dance as follows:

> "In the evening I went to the fandango, at the invitation of the mayor, and met with a merry and happy hearted set. They all danced, and scarce a moment during the evening but what the floor was occupied with couples whirling in the graceful waltz. They danced the 'cumbe,' they waltzed and danced again. The alcalde and his wife sat at the head of the room; she had a black bottle full of aguardiente and this she dealt to the most honored; and a peasant went around the room selling apples. The music was

produced by guitars, violins, and voices. The singers composed their songs impromptu; and often the listeners would burst forth into lengthened peals of laughter at some happy stroke of witty improvisation." (Walter 1916:21)

Another favorite game was <u>canutes</u>. About twenty people would gather in a room and one was chosen to hide the <u>canutes</u>. These were four short lengths of cane eight to ten inches long and marked with different symbols by a hot wire. The person chosen hid the <u>canutes</u>, one in each pile of dirt heaped in each corner of the room, placing them so that the unmarked ends protruded above the dirt and all the time holding a blanket before him to hide his motions from the others. Another variation was to require the participants to leave the room in which the person hid the <u>canutes</u>. When finished he blew a flute to call them back into the room. One participant then started the game by pulling one canute from a dirt pile. If he drew the <u>Mulato</u> he lost ten grains of corn and if it was the <u>Cinchado</u>, he won ten grains. The <u>Uno</u> or <u>Dos</u> lost five grains. One informant stated , however, that the <u>Mulato</u> was worth ten grains. The value of the grains of corn was that agreed upon by the participants. Sometimes, a grain would be worth a goat or a cow in a high stakes game. The winner was next in turn to hide the <u>canutes</u>. While the game was being played special songs were sung. Below are two examples:

El Uno es mi conocido.   The One is best-known to me.
El Dos es mi defensor.   The Two is my defender.
El Cinchado es mi amigo   The Belted One is my friend
Y el Mulato es un traidor.   And the Mulatto is a traitor.
Anda picale el Mulato,   Go pickup up the Mulato,
Mulato pagador.   Mulato the payer.

El hombre José Torres   The man José Torres
Se le seco la Pirata.   The Pirate didn't come through for him
¿Que dicen los Mirabales   What do the Mirabales say
Que esta noche   That tonight
Le echan la riata?   Will "throw the rope"?

Another popular gambling game was _pelota_. Three flat rectangular sticks, marked on one face were used. They were held in the hand and then thrown together on the floor much in the same way as dice. If they all fell with the marked faces on the bottom the thrower won ten grains of corn from the man he was betting with. If the marked faces appear on the top he lost ten grains of corn. Two marks up lost five and two marks down won five.

In _bolas_ a similar gambling game four clay balls were used, one with three encircling bands, one with a hole through it, the third with a depression, and the last pierced with three holes. The balls were thrown together into a corner of a room, their position determining the winner and the amount he won.

Tejas was a game similar to quoits. Four small discs were thrown at holes in the ground and the score varied with the number that went into the holes. Culin notes a similar game of quoits played at Zuni Indian Pueblo but whether there was a relationship or just coincidence has not been determined (1902-1903:727).

Sueco, a popular game, was similar to "shinny" played by the Anglo-Americans. The implements consisted of curved oak sticks and a small ball of tough cowhide. At either end of the field lines were drawn for goals. The game began with the ball and the majority of players in the center of the field, although a few players were stationed as defense near the goal lines. The first team won that knocked the ball with the curved sticks across the goal line of the other team. This game is similar to one played throughout the Rio Grande Indian Pueblos (Culin 1902-1903:642-643).

Another game played at Manzano is mentioned in the _Gringo and Greaser_, December 1, 1883, as follows:

"Juan Cordova of the Aurora had his finger broken in the game called 'Lucha del Dedo'. This sapient sport consists in the contestants' locking a finger, generally the middle finger - - and testing who is the better man. They don't play this game when the fool killer is about."

An old Spanish game was <u>la jura</u>. At fiesta time and on saints' days a man with money took a handful of change and told small children to gather around him. Then he threw the money into the air, exclaiming, "I am throwing the money to <u>La Jura</u>." The children then scrambled for the money. No fighting was permitted.

During the early period of Anglo-American acculturation there seems to have been a small efflorescence of native culture in the region. For example, poems, songs, riddles and proverbs were composed during this period. The best known of the regional artists, however, did not live in Manzano but at the neighboring village of Torreón. This poet, Casamiro Lujan, wrote many ballads, proverbs, and riddles describing the life of Spanish-Americans of the Estancia Valley. Below are a few of his selections:

<u>Es palabra de Jesús Cristo y de Dios padre aprobada quien sera aquel mas contento que el que no desea nada</u>. Translation: It is approved word of Jesus Christ and God the praised father that who can be more content than he who desires nothing.

<u>Midete con la riqueza y no te acabalaras y midete con la pobreza y de todo te sobrara</u>. Translation: Measure yourself with richness and you won't have enough and measure yourself with poverty and you will have plenty left over.

Ay del que en el alma encierra las cenizas de su amor,
Ay del que vive llevando la muerte en el corazon,
Ay del que ahora perdida la ventura que sono,
Ay del que su amor confia a una mujer sin amor,
Porque para el ya no tiene ni rayo la luz del sol,
Ni colores las campinas ni grato aroma la flor.

Free translation of the above poem   follows:

Alas, the soul shut up by the ashes of your love,
Alas, those who live carrying death in the heart,
Alas, those who now lost the fortune that rings through the air,
Alas, those that confide their lives in a women without love,
Because to him the sun no longer sheds its rays,
Nor have the fields their colors nor flowers their pleasant aroma.

Other songs and ballads remembered at Manzano include the "Indita de Amado Chavez" (Appendix V), "The Indita de Manuel B. Otero" (Appendix VII) and "El Borracho" [The drunkard] (Appendix VI). At Manzano the poet, Dionicio Garcia, wrote a poem titled "Chapulin" [grasshopper]) telling about a grasshopper plague that occurred in the area in 1866. The telling of riddles was also a popular activity at Manzano (Appendix VIII) as were recounting events about the supernatural.

A description of the traditional marriage customs at Manzano is contained in the Gringo and Greaser, December 1, 1883. It states:

"Mexican betrothals and marriages are of a primitive fashion, recalling vividly the customs of the Jews in the times of Abraham and Sarah, Isaac and Rebecca, Jacob and Rachael. The young folks have little to say in the selection of their life partners; the old people arranging the whole business to suit themselves. Previous to the betrothal the young couple may not even be acquainted. They seem to act upon the theory that a wife's a wife and a husband's a husband, for all that Mexican couples seem to be as well mated as are others. The church regulates the laws of marriage among them and permits no divorces; it is truly for better or worse and that as long as both shall live."

The following three items from the same issue of the Gringo and Greaser depicts other aspects of the traditional Manzano culture:

"A belief prevails among the Mexicans that babies do not receive their sight until they are baptized."

"The Mexican style of butter making is childlike and bland. They make it with a spoon for a dasher and a tin pan for a churn, and it isn't firkin butter either. They set the pan o' milk in cool water and then with the spoon beat or agitate the milk a la eggnog, and lo! the cow lard appears. They don't make enough to glut the market at a churning, or spooning, but is butter all the same, and none of your dog-on butterine or oleomargarine either."

"Much time was spent in formal and informal gatherings of family and friends in their respective homes."

The wide variety of leisure-time activities and social games gives evidence that during the early period of Anglo-American acculturation a high degree of traditional cultural patterns and social self-sufficiency was preserved.

Manzano in the last century had acquired among some people a reputation for criminality. For example, Major Carleton mentions this aspect in 1855. One local story tells of a man from Tomé who came to Manzano with an oxcart of apples for sale. While there his oxen were stolen. He left town to recover them and when he returned after an unsuccessful chase, his apples too had been stolen. In anger he composed this poem:

Que bonito es el Manzano	How beautiful is Manzano
Con sus verdes sementaras,	With its green fields.
Con sus bosques y maderas,	With its forests and woods.
Todos los tiene en la mano.	All these it has at hand.
Que bonito es el Manzano,	How beautiful is Manzano,
Que en el lugar de llevar dejo	So let him who is a so-and-and so
Asi vuelva a las Manzanas aquel	Return to the apple trees.
Que fuera pendejo.	
Hermosos de vinas de llanos,	Beautiful vineyards and plains
Porque me voy y las dejo,	Because I am going I leave you it.
Volvere venir a Manzano,	I will return to Manzano
Asi que soy un pendejo.	Even though I be a so-and-so.

Summary

In summary, during the period of Anglo-American acculturation in the last century there were several major changes in Manzano culture even though the effects were not spread evenly over all aspects of their culture. When Lieutenant Abert entered in Manzano in 1846 he was well received and he had no criticism for the culture of the inhabitants but Major Carleton entering the village in 1855 received a hostile reception and he was full of criticism about the moral status of the inhabitants. It is difficult, however, to accept the conclusions that in only nine years moral degradation had set in.

The traditional role in community organization was further weakened by the forbidding of slavery and peonage. In the last decades of the past century community integration and self-sufficiency was weakened by the forbidding of the Penitente Organization by Padre Sembrano. Nevertheless, Americans such as Charles Kusz and Johnson moved into the community. Kusz set up a newspaper indicating the continued importance of Manzano in the Estancia Valley. Mining engineers moved in and expedited the mining industry. Political control shifted from Mexico to the United States. Danger from the Navajo warriors gradually disappeared as the United States Army rounded them up in 1880 and forced them to move to Fort Sumner to the east of the Estancia Valley. As a result the local militia, which had served as an integrating factor in community life, was no longer needed.

In spite of all these outside influences on Manzano culture many traditional cultural traits such as agricultural methods, social customs, recreational activities, handicrafts and artistic endeavors continued.

CHAPTER V

THE PERIOD Of INTENSE ACCULTURATION WITH AMERICAN CULTURE, 1900-1938

During 1902-1903 the first railroad, the Santa Fe Central, now called the New Mexico Central, was extended into the Estancia Valley. This railroad ran from Santa Fe through Moriarity, Estancia, Willard, Progresso and Torrance. Several years later it was connected at Torrance with the El Paso Southwestern, a branch of the Southern Pacific Railway (Las Nuevas de Estancia, November 25, 1904). The effects of the railroad was that of bringing homesteaders, business men, and travelers into the Estancia Valley. In addition, the demand for ties stimulated the Manzano lumber business.

In the past century when Manzano was in Valencia County the Manzaneños who needed to conduct business in the Court House had to make a long trip to the Rio Grande Valley. In 1903 the County of Torrance was created out of the eastern part of Valencia County. Many of the people of Manzano objected to its boundaries and name. According to Las Nuevas de Estancia November 25, 1904:

"Monday we had the privilege of spending the day at Manzano. We were well received by all. The people commented on the way Las Nuevas has talked of preserving the historical things in the county of Torrance.

"Speaking of the new county they expressed their opinion that the boundaries should be changed, especially the west one. There are people who live on this side of the mountains who desire to enter the new county. Now they have to cross the mountains and travel many miles to go to their county seat and some have the idea that the name of the county should be changed to Manzano as this is a more significant name. The Manzano Mountains are named from the

79

town and for this reason the name has some worth. The old plaza of Manzano is loved by the old people and this is a desireable name for the county.

"The town should petition to the legislature to change these boundaries and the name."

For the people who lived in Manzano the establishment of Torrance County and the county seat at Estancia facilitated their legal and political relations, for they no longer had to travel over the mountains to the county seat of Valencia County, Los Lunas.

In the beginning of this century several Americans moved into Manzano and were responsible for changes in the life of the Manzaneños. For example, a medical doctor named Amble moved to the village in 1904 and remained there until 1914. Before this doctor there was another one residing in Manzano. Presenting a cross section of process of acculturation are the life stories of Tenos Tabet and I. K. McKinley.

Tenos Tabet was born in Syria in 1869, coming to the United states with his brother in 1891. He stayed in this country until 1901 when he returned to Syria and married. The next year he returned to the United States and moved from Albuquerque to Manzano by wagon. Having at that time a capital of $4,000 he opened a general store, selling $600 worth of merchandise the first year and making a profit of $1,000 dealing in hides and pelts. The following year, Tabet was about to move to Albuquerque when he heard that Eugenio Romero had a contract to make 1,500,000 ties for the Santa Fe Railroad to be extended through Abó Pass. All timber was to be cut near Manzano. As a result a boom began and Tabet remained. Soon five sawmills were operating near Manzano, owned and operated by Romero, Frankenburger and Spencer and by Dunn, manager for Gross, Kelly & Company of Albuquerque. In a single year of this period Tabet's profit was $10,000 derived mainly from the millworkers. The only other store in Manzano was owned by Eleno Zamora.

In 1908 Eugenio Romero persuaded McKinley to take over his mill and later McKinley bought the mills of Dunn and Spencer. McKinley describes the lumber industry as follows:

> "The mills were all small, moving from canyon to canyon in the Manzano Mountains as the supply was exhausted in each location. The best grade lumber was usually contracted for by Gross, Kelly & Company. Ties were sold to the Santa Fe Railroad. Other grades of lumber were sold to individuals. The timber was hauled by local Spanish-Americans furnishing their own teams, wagons and feed and receiving their pay every Saturday night by the thousand board feet hauled. Rarely were the lumber workers without money in their pockets".

Until 1932, when the mills were sold to his sons, McKinley was one of Manzano's chief employers. Nearly all the men at this village worked for him one time or the other.

In addition to stimulating an economic boom at Manzano the lumber and retail business aided in the preservation of some of the aspects of the traditional peon-patrón system, although now it was an Anglo-American and a Syrian who were the patrones. McKinley and Tabet testify to the extreme extent to which their laborers depended upon them for advice, information, and social and economic betterment.

Manzano was slowly becoming a major center for business activities for the entire Estancia Valley. Tabet used to send as many as twenty-five to thirty wagons to Albuquerque for supplies and to carry his hides and pelts, since he also was a purchaser of these items. However, the trading business in time proved hazardous and the preeminence it gave Manzano was transitory.

The Estancia Valley was opened to homesteading in 1905 in the portion of the old land grant to Governor Bartolome Baca but it was not until 1909 that the region was intensively homesteaded, with the result that large areas of good grazing land still remained for a few

years. According to informants, in 1909 Tabet owned nearly 3,000 sheep
and in time owned 160,000, although this number seems exaggerated.

In 1905 the Territory of New Mexico claimed $1,600 in back taxes
from the inhabitants of the Manzano Grant. The five Land Grant
Commissioners came to Tabet to ask if he could pay the amount since at
that time the townsmen did not have sufficient funds. Shortage of cash
at that time may have been caused by the seasonal nature of work at the
lumber mills although it may have been the result of the workers
spending their money as fast as they were paid, often having little
available when debts arose. Tabet agreed and paid the taxes. Later he
collected four dollars from each man owning 40 acres which nearly repaid
the loan. By selling some land he made up the deficit. The lumber mills
continued to bring large amounts of money to town and the workers in
time were able to pay their taxes.

With the establishment of Torrance County and the influx of the
homesteaders Manzano was brought into much closer contact with the
Anglo-American culture. Nevertheless, the initial entrance of the
homesteaders and other Anglo-Americans was not reflected to any great
extent in the population growth of Manzano. In fact, the first peak was
reached in 1860 and from then on there was a gradual decline until 1910
when there was a slow rise in population until 1940 caused not by the
movement of many Anglo-Americans but by the prosperity of new economic
activities such as the lumber industry and possibly by increase in
public health programs. These population figures are shown below:

TABLE 1

POPULATION OF MANZANO, PUNTA DE AGUA, AND TAJIQUE (U. S. CENSUS)

Year	Manzano	Punta de Agua	Tajique
1850	403	( )*	( )*
1860	831	237	351
1870	738	338	534
1880	( )*	( )*	( )*
1890	658	290	350
1900	649	100	318
1910	607	632	738
1920	752	318	325
1930	708	393	399
1940	812	414	373
1950	434	215	297

* Not recorded

Torrance County can be classified as rural, for the only city over 1,000 in population is Mountainair, which had 1,477 inhabitants in 1940. It is from this community and Estancia, the county seat, that the main Anglo-American cultural traits are diffused to Manzano. Mountainair and the other primarily Anglo-American communities in the Estancia Valley have witnessed a steady decline in population since 1910.

Of all the cultural traits introduced into the Estancia Valley, the development of the pinto bean as a cash crop and the consequent shrinking of land for livestock production have had a major effect upon Manzano economics. Mr. I. K. McKinley, who was later to become a lumberman at Manzano, explains how a market was found for the Estancia Valley pinto beans. He had been a lumberman previously in Oklahoma but swore he would never follow this profession again. Entering in a blinding snowstorm in 1905 he established his claim for a homestead near Tajique. The following year there was a big meeting of farmers who were raising pinto beans in the Estancia Valley, for they had not been able to sell their crop. They agreed to donate beans from their next crop and a man was chosen to travel throughout the country until he had given away all these beans. The beans were cooked and flavored with meat. McKinley donated 100 lbs. of beans. Thus, the market was established.

The raising of the pinto bean itself, or at least beans, had a long history in the region even before the Anglo-Americans began producing them. For example, at the nearby Quarai Pueblo ruins, many charred beans were encountered in the excavation project of 1939-1940. When the Spanish-Americans entered the area they continued the production of the bean. At Manzano and other nearby Spanish-American communities, however, beans were raised for local consumption in contrast to the Anglo-Americans who produced for the market. Once a market was found for beans the Manzaneños produced a small amount for a cash income.

The loss of land for livestock forced the people of Manzano to turn to agriculture as a primary source of income. They continued following for a long time their traditional and primitive methods of farming. McKinley describes the techniques for agriculture as follows: when he first came to Manzano, the local farmers turned the ground with a home-made plow drawn by oxen, while behind them followed a man throwing beans into the tilled land by hand. When beans had pushed above ground, the men, women and children cultivated the plants with wide-bladed home-made hoes. Thrashing was still done by beating the dried plants with sticks or having horses or oxen walk over them. The beans sold on the market at $1.00 to $1.50 per hundred pounds. McKinley states that he saw piles of corn in town as high as a house which if true would indicate that the Manzaneños were producing a surplus of this crop for a cash income.

Manzano continued to have a reputation for criminality. In the early 1900s there was only one deputy in the village, the sheriff being stationed at Los Lunas, county seat for Valencia County. Several people of notorious character are said to have lived in Manzano, the worst being a bandit named Padilla. On one occasion several sheriffs and deputies pursued him. As they drew near he stationed himself on a hill near the village. He challenged them to come near him but they left. In 1909 2,265 sheep were stolen from Tabet during the lambing season. He spent a great of amount of money trying to trace the thieves but failed. According to rumors the stolen stock was taken to a man in the White Mountains who paid a dollar per sheep. Later "this fence" went bankrupt but was never apprehended.

Another example of crime concerned the murder of a child north of the nearby Red Canyon. This boy was attacked by a group of men from Manzano while herding sheep and the stock was stolen. The thieves slit the boy's throat and buried him among rocks. After the body decayed it was discovered by a dog belonging to a Spanish-American who lived nearby. This man reported the find and an investigation was held. The murderers could not be identified. According to informants, a band of horse thieves, led by a man from Manzano, also operated out of Manzano.

During the days of Prohibition several Manzaneños and inhabitants of nearby villages engaged in the bootlegging business. A large still occupied in 1939 a side room of the main Manzano dance hall. In several canyons in the nearby Manzano Mountains where spring water was available the Manzaneños operated stills. Near the Quarai Pueblo ruins some of the residents of Punta de Agua stored the finished product in barrels buried underground.

Manzano beginning in this century became involved in political scandals. An example is reported in the Estancia News of 1904,

"The first Republican Convention was held in Manzano on October 1, 1904. Colonel J. Franco Chavez called the convention to order and was made chairman. Trouble started over a proposal to appoint a committee of one from each precinct as nominators. Several people objected to the proposal but could gain no recognition; furthermore, the appointed committee could not agree among themselves. Finally, twenty-five of the forty-nine delegates walked out and called a convention at Punta de Agua, October 5th. After several days they nominated an independent ticket and a few days later Colonel Chavez was found murdered."

According to the Estancia News Herald, June 15, 1939,

"...in reading this bit of ancient history, it is plain to be seen that here is where the fight started which finally culminated in the assassination of Col. Chavez."

Juan Arroyos was a bandit who lived in Punta de Agua. At that time there were French trappers and prospectors in New Mexico. Arroyos went to the Gallina Mountains and murdered two of these prospectors for their possessions. Pablo Jones, the constable of Punta de Agua, apprehended Arroyos and on the way back to Punta de Agua, rather than taking the prisoner to Los Lunas, killed him near Quarai. He claimed that Arroyos tried to escape. Arroyos was buried in the Quarai Mission.

Aurelio Chavez claims that the Manzaneños hold a grudge against him. During the last election his son was shot at one night. He tried to find the man who did the shooting and when encountered Aurelio was also fired at. A struggle ensued between the two men and Aurelio and his son were able to wrest the gun from the other man. The case was tried in the court in Estancia. The man was fined $15.00 and released. Later the fine was suspended. Another time while Aurelio was walking in the forest someone shot at him three times. The culprit was later arrested and sentenced to the state penitentiary for seven years.

In summary, many major changes occurred in Manzano culture during the first three decades of this century, resulting from the influence of the Anglo-Americans. Primarily, Manzano lost much of its autonomy as it became integrated into the New Mexico political system. The county seat was changed from Los Lunas in Valencia County to Estancia in Torrance

County, which because of the shorter distance to be traveled made the legal and political business to be more easily expedited. The main traditional industry of livestock raising lost its place to agriculture as the homesteaders fenced the range of the Estancia Valley for the cultivation of the pinto bean. At Manzano beans were also cultivated but now not only for local subsistence but for a cash income. The rise in importance of the lumber industry combined with the need for money to buy essentials at the stores operated by Tabet and Romero also stimulated the need for a cash income. Manzano's reputation for harboring criminals continued. The importance of Manzano in the life of the Estancia Valley was witnessed by its being a trade center and the fact that the first Republican Convention was held here.

CHAPTER VI

MANZANO IN THE POST-1930 PERIOD

Introduction

The period beginning in 1930 at Manzano was marked by the effects
of the Great Depression beginning in 1929 and the onset of the droughts
of the 1930s. Both these events resulted in a serious economic crisis at
Manzano followed by the incorporation of the villagers into the various
public welfare programs, the end result being an acceleration of the
disorganization of traditional culture.

The Present-day Manzaneños; Physical Description

As with any group of people it is impossible to make
generalizations regarding their physical structure that will apply to
every individual. The typical individual of Spanish-American descent has
a dark complexion, brown eyes, straight to curly black hair, and medium
height and weight. Many individuals in their facial appearance have
American Indian traits such as broad cheekbones, rounded faces and blue-
black, straight hair, characteristics to be expected because of their
large amount of blood from this race. Several Spanish-American men and
women in the village, however, have blue or green eyes, and red,
blonde, or light-brown hair characteristic of the "Gallegos" (according
to local informants, descendants of Spaniards from Galicia) or people

born outside of Manzano. Among the 366 individuals registered in the voting files the latter characteristics were present in ten male and four female Spanish-Americans, five Syrians, six Anglo-Americans, and one mixed Spanish-French. Several of the Spanish-Americans claim to have traces of Irish and other North European blood.

An investigation I made of the weight of the Manzaneños over twenty-five years old revealed that 138 men averaged 156 pounds and 185 women, 113.9; the medium weight of the men, 138.45 and women, 100.9; and the mode 128.5 for men and 98.5 for women. The weight range among the males varied from 96 to 209 pounds; among women, 75 to 175 lbs.

Average height for men was five feet seven inches; for women, five feet three inches; medium height for males, five feet five inches; for females, five feet two inches. Mode for males was five feet six inches; for females, five feet three inches. Range among men was five feet to six feet two inches; for women, four feet six inches to five feet six inches. The men of Manzano average heavier that the average weight of all the United States army recruits of World War I (Harris, and Jackson 1930:83). The Manzaneños also are taller than the average male of central Spain who average five feet three inches and in fact their height is equal to that of the English people in a study made by Ripley (1889:96). Thus, there is no evidence that the inhabitants of Manzano are malnourished or suffering from physical deterioration.

Ethnic composition of the 366 registered voters include 342 Spanish-Americans, 11 Anglo-Americans, 5 Syrians and 8 mixed Spanish-French. Among the Spanish-Americans it is not possible to determine the amount of their American Indian blood. The mixed French-Spanish inhabitants are descended from people who migrated from Taos, while the resident priest is of French descent. One of the local Anglo-Americans is married to a Spanish-American woman.

Of the 96 Spanish-Americans born outside of Manzano, 69% of men and 68% of women came from a 100 mile radius; none came from outside of New Mexico. It is noteworthy that all the Anglo-Americans were born outside of the 100 mile limit. These figures probably indicate that Spanish-Americans when they move tend to migrate to other communities that have a high percent of Spanish-Americans. Appendix X shows the place of birth of the Manzaneños.

According to the U. S. Census the population in 1930 was almost evenly divided by sex for there were 356 men and 352 women of a total of 708. In this group were 704 native-born of native parents and four of foreign-born parentage. In 1950 Manzano had a larger percentage of males, 214, compared with 189 females, possibly because of female mortality in child birth. In 1870 Manzano had five foreign-born inhabitants in contrast to none in 1930.

Household composition

As defined here the term "household" refers to a group of individuals who live in a single house and eat from the same table. The table on the next page shows the household composition of 115 Manzano households that I surveyed.

This table indicates that the largest group of households, 59.2%, are composed of nuclear families, that is a married couple and their children. The next largest group are married couples without children, 8%. All other types vary from 4% to .08%. According to informants the traditional household at one time included the three generations, that is a married couple, their parents, and children. If this be true there has been a major change through time in the composition of the Manzano households.

TABLE II

CLASSIFICATION OF HOUSEHOLDS AT MANZANO

Unit	Number
1. Man, wife and children......................................	74
2. Man, wife and no children..................................	10
3. Man, wife and adopted children............................	6
4. Man, wife, children and adopted children..................	2
5. Widow and children..	3
6. Widow and adopted children................................	4
7. Widower and adopted children..............................	3
8. Widower, children and adopted children....................	1
9. Father living with married couple.........................	3
10. Mother living with married couple........................	6
11. Mother living with two married couples...................	1
12. Married man's wife living with father....................	1
13. Unmarried man living with father and nephew..............	1
14. Son living with mother and adopted child.................	1
15. Single working man living alone..........................	1
16. Widow living alone.......................................	1
17. Mother and father living with married couple.............	1
18. Married couple, married son, single son and single sister....1	
19. Blind man living with an unrelated married couple............1	
20. Feeble-minded man living with an unrelated married couple....1	
21. Married couple, mother, brother, sister and nephew...........1	
22. Two unrelated families living together (total of 7 children).2	
Total households.........125	

Households vary considerably in size, averaging 4.52 members, with a range from one to twelve and a median of four. The Table III on the next page shows the size of households:

Eighty-seven households have children, 294 or 69.6% including 149 boys and 135 girls. If the children are added by sex to the adult registered voters, males at Manzano outnumber females, a distribution noted as early as 1870. The average number of children per household is 3.2% this figure being taken from households with natural rather than adopted children. Greatest number of children in one family was 25 and the largest number of children living in any one household was 10. In the total number of children per household the one family with the 25 children was not included in the total because these children were living in several different households.

TABLE III

FREQUENCY OF HOUSEHOLD SIZE

Number in household	Examples

```
1...........................................4
2..........................................17
3..........................................22
4..........................................24
5..........................................17
6..........................................14
7..........................................14
8...........................................4
9...........................................7
10..........................................0
11..........................................1
12..........................................1
              Total households......125
```

During the years, 1939-1940, according to the files of the Works Projects Administration Office in Estancia, in the Manzano households there were 26 examples of adoption which included 9 granddaughters, 9 grandsons, 2 cousins, 2 nephews, 2 nieces and 2 who were not related to the guardians, indicating that the greatest number were relatives. The reasons given for adoption were: (1) grandmother old and living alone and thus needed help of granddaughter, (2) mother of child died when it was a baby and the grandparents adopted it, (3) sons given to grandparents because there were too many in the parental households to support them, (4) children given to grandparents so they would have company and (5) two boys placed in a family by the Department of Public Welfare. According to local informants it is a Spanish-American custom to give children to grandparents if they need their help.

Housing

Family life centers in the home at Manzano. In a survey of the houses I found that many of the dwellings are built side by side and give the appearance of long rambling structures (Figures XIV-XVI). Nevertheless, the units of these compound dwellings were counted as separate houses when each held a distinct household and were constructed at different times. Ninety-seven houses were present in the village in 1939-1940, excluding stores, dance halls, cantinas, sheds and outhouses. The most common type of dwellings was the casa de latas or jacal, of which there were 68, or 71% of the total. In this group were 14 flat-roofed or sotella type of houses, 19.7, 11 with gabled wood roofs and 47 with tin roofs, indicating the persistence of local house types (Figures XII-XIII). Here were also three abandoned stone houses, each with a tin roof. There was also only one log house, the fuerte type. One of the storekeepers owned the only newer type of Spanish-American type of houses, that is one made of adobe and with the walls plastered with stucco. Although the jacal is the most common house type it is not preferred since the base of the vertical wall posts rot. Nevertheless, since it is easy to build it is the most common variety. In building the jacal pine poles are preferred and straight poles of juniper and pinyon are second choice.

In general the fronts of the houses are painted various colors such as green, blue, yellow or brown colors over the mud-plastered walls. Several houses have open porches and a few have screened ones, the latter being a non-traditional type. Screens, however, are common on windows, wood shutters being extremely rare. A large portion of the furnishings are homemade. Wall paper is made of newspapers although some

of the more "modern" houses are decorated with commercial wallpaper. In
nearly all houses are statues of saints and other religious objects made
of plaster of paris. Other forms of interior decorations include
calenders, framed photographs, colored advertisements and nick-knacks
such as plaster of paris animals bought at local fairs. In one house
long strings of bottle caps served as window curtains. Christmas tree
decorations such as tinsel and balls are left in some houses all year
long. Rugs are usually made from twisted rags. Most of the houses are
very clean and their yards are constantly swept. Surrounding the houses
are fences of wire, stone or wood pickets. Garden flowers are rare and
when present consist of hollyhocks and morning glories. In fact a large
number of the homes and yards are kept cleaner than their inhabitants.

According to the files of the Works Projects Administration office
in Estancia the average number of persons, shown in the table in the
Appendix XI, is 1.07 person per room. The small number indicates that
over-crowding is not present in all the houses. Nevertheless, there are
some over-crowded houses such as that of the family of nine that lives
in a two-room house.

Associated with the houses are sheds, barns, corrals and outhouses.
A complete account was not made since most were compound structures and
it was difficult to define a unit. A sample of 59 of these structures
was made to obtain an idea of their construction. Twenty-four were made
of planks and wood slabs; 23 were made of logs, the fuerte construction,
10 were jacals and 4 made of adobe.

Hay and corn fodder are stored on top of the above types of
outbuildings or on tapeistes, the latter a four pole framework with a
cross beam top. Corrals are made of planks or upright planks while those
made of criss-crossed logs are rare. Outhouses are constructed of planks

and often are unsanitary. Many houses have the beehive-shaped outdoor ovens (hornos) and iron grills, the latter being used to heat barrels of water for washing. Plank-covered wells are common.

An investigation of home ownership of 125 households revealed that 109 homes, 87%, were owned by the household head; 4 belong to the married man's father; 2 to the father-in-law; 1 to the mother; 1 to the nephew; 1 to a daughter; 1 to a son; 1 to a granddaughter and only 5 to unrelated individuals. All 16 houses belonging to individuals other than the household head were rent-free since renting houses is not a Manzano custom.

Toward the institution of marriage Manzaneños show a profound respect, an attitude reinforced by their strong Roman Catholic Church convictions. In addition, one of the primary desires of these people is to be married and settle down to family life. Consequently, marriage is encouraged at an early age. In 125 households investigated the youngest married man was 19; the youngest married woman, 15, of which there were 3 examples, while the next youngest man was 21. Nine married women were also under 21. According to local customs the ideal time for men to marry is between 18 to 20 years and for women between 17 and 18. That there is sentiment towards and early marriage was expressed by the frequency in which they asked me why I had not married, when was I going to get married and by the frequent comments that I should hurry up and obtain a wife.

Figures for the 366 registered voters in the Manzano precinct indicate that 240 were married Spanish Americans; 38, widows, 9, unmarried women; and 51, unmarried men, including widowers and men who had not married. Because of the strong Roman Catholic convictions divorce is rare, there being only one divorced person in Manzano.

Women customarily marry men considerably older than themselves. Of
125 households I investigated the men averaged 6.9 years older than the
women. In this group the men averaged 44.4 years and the women, 37.5.
Only 12 women in the 92 married couples were older than their
husbands. One man was 29 years older than his wife while in another
couple the difference was 13 years, the man being 71 years old and the
woman, 58.

Marriage is preceded by a period of courtship. There is now no
standardized pattern. "Dates" in the Anglo-American form are not common
for it is unusual to have young men and women who are approaching
marriageable age be seen together as a couple. Trysts are uncommon for
even at dances young men arrive and leave in the company of other men
and likewise so do the young women. In lieu of these customs the young
people usually become acquainted by more casual means such as meeting
each other in churches and during family visits to one another's homes.
In 1939, however, these traditional Spanish-American customs were
beginning to change. Those young men who owned cars often followed the
Anglo-American customs of "dating", sometimes taking the girls to dances
in nearby towns and villages. The acquisition of automobiles seems to be
a strong factor in changing the courtship pattern of Manzano culture.

Usually the courtship period is soon followed by marriage while
long periods of engagement, which often occur among Anglo-Americans, are
rare. Factors responsible for the latter custom, such as inability to
find work or provide for a family, do not seem to retard Manzano
marriages. The mores associated with the preliminaries to marriages have
changed considerably since the time of Lieutenant Abert's visit in 1846
when the betrothals were arranged by the parents, often without the
young couples' wishes. The approved customs today involve these

proceedings: when a man finds the girl he wants to marry he expresses his intention to his father. His father, mother or grandparents visit the family of the girl and announces the young man's intentions. Occasionally this custom is varied by a member of the boy's family writing a letter to the girl's parents. The girl's family does not give their answer upon reception of the boy's parents or his letter. Instead they wait several days to answer. If the answer is "No" the Manzaneños call this response <u>dando las calabazas</u> [giving the pumpkins]. If the answer is "Yes" a ceremony called the <u>prendorio</u> [getting acquainted] is given. This is a party and feast held at the house of the girl's parents and is literally, as the name indicates, a getting acquainted ceremony. All the relatives of the young man's and young woman's parents are invited so that they can know each other. The guests are usually restricted to members of the families. At this feast the boy gives the girl an engagement ring, obligating them to go through with a marriage contract. This ceremony has the secondary function of announcing to the village the approaching marriage. If the boy can afford it a dance is given at night and all are invited. At the dance delicacies are served such as cookies and candy. Sometimes several musicians are hired to provide entertainment. In these ceremonies the main change is that although the parents no longer select the marriage partners it is still necessary to obtain the consent of the girl's parents. As a compromise some Manzaneños first make the decision themselves to get married and then go through the older formality of asking consent of the girl's parents. All the marriages, however, that were known to me followed the more formal pattern given above.

After the <u>prendorio</u>, announcement of the approaching marriage is given to the local priest, who sets a date for the marriage to occur about two weeks later. The fee charged is $12.00. Then the prospective bride and groom go to confession, for it is not the custom to confess on a day of a dance (usually held after the wedding ceremony). Before the marriage the man and his family must buy the wedding dress for his bride. If he believes or knows she is a virgin he presents to her a crown and veil to be used during the marriage; if he knows or suspects differently he buys only the long bridal dress. Although the function is not to announce to the public the bride's status this is the actual result. This custom is strongly adhered to for it is a religious belief that only virgins can wear a crown and veil. A non-virgin would not dare to defy this custom since it would negate her strong religious convictions.

After the church ceremony the married couple goes to the house of the bride's parents to celebrate a feast called the fiesta de casorio to which relatives and close friends are invited. Musicians are hired to provide entertainment. The feast starts about noon with the refresco consisting of alcoholic drinks, cookies, candies and other refreshments. After everyone is served they gather around and talk, congratulating the young people while the musicians play. About a half hour later dinner is served with the guests sitting first. After dinner the talking, singing and music are resumed. Occasionally at this time the groom gives the bride the wedding ring; sometimes it is given in church. If the groom can afford it a dance is held in the afternoon in the local dance hall. Afterwards everybody returns to the house for more conversation and music. About six o'clock la cena [supper] is served with everyone remaining until the formal wedding dance, la baile de casorio, is held.

If the boy or his family are too poor or if his or her parents are in mourning no dance is given; instead, it is customary for the bride, groom, their relatives and their friends to walk around Manzano singing with musical accompaniment. This custom is called <u>sacando</u> <u>el</u> <u>gallo</u> [bringing out the rooster]. The same term is applied to the custom whereby the musicians walk around the village about three o'clock in the afternoon announcing a free dance.

Everyone may attend a wedding dance and it is usually so crowded that some of the people must remain outside the open door. At about seven-thirty or eight o'clock those who attended the afternoon ceremonies in the bride's house appear at the dance. The bride and groom occupy seats directly in front of the musicians' platform. The dance begins with the formal wedding march led by a man and woman familiar with the steps. In a variant I witnessed at Punta de Agua the bride's father and the bride were the first to dance. Next were the married couple dancing together. All couples in the room then join, marching side by side in a long line. Then the leading couple stop, hold up their hands and the end couples in sequence march through, a figure similar to the Virginia Reel. In turn when this couple passes under the arms they in turn stop and hold up their arms. This figure is formed several times or at least until everyone in the room has participated. Afterwards the couples break apart and dance separately face to face. Anyone can cut in.

At about midnight the dance breaks up and the married couple, relatives and invited guests again sojourn to the home of the bride's parents. Then, the wedding cake is cut by the four godparents of the bride and groom and served to the guests together with other refreshments. This part of the ceremony is called <u>El</u> <u>cafe</u>. After the food has been served an old man familiar with marriage customs gives a talk about one hour in length to the newly-wed couple, exhorting them to

be faithful to one another and impressing them with their
responsibilities and religious duties. At the end of this talk the
musicians play for a short time and thus is concluded the marriage
ceremony. These customs seem to be general through the Spanish-American
cultures of the Southwest (Scott, 1923:79-80).

Because of their strong Roman Catholic convictions divorce is a
rare phenomenon at Manzano. In fact only one example of divorce was
encountered in a survey I made of 125 households. Remarriage after
death, however, is permitted. In this survey there were seven men and
one woman remarried and two men and one woman had remarried twice. In
these households there were, however, nine widows and six widowers.

Desire for children is strong and I could find no evidence of the
use of contraceptives. Eighty-seven households, 70% of the 125 total,
had children. This did not include 18 households with adopted children.
Only ten families consisted of man and wife without children while one
family had 25 children.

No figures were obtained on the types of childbirths that occurred
at Manzano. In Torrance County, according the the New Mexico Department
of Health, which includes more than Manzano, in 1937 there were 48
births, 8 of which were attended by a physician, 32 by midwives and 1 by
a member of the family.

At Manzano a typical delivery is to have a midwife give a woman in
labor a cup of tea while the woman herself prays and mutters such
exclamations as "A Dios" [Oh God] when stricken with pain. Sometimes the
more religious people hang a cross at the foot of the bed to invoke the
saints. The relatives usually gather in the room at this time, praying
constantly. A brew made of the wild herb culantro is given to the newborn baby. After birth, according to local informants, the woman is

confined to bed about ten days. I observed, however, a woman washing clothes three days after giving birth while another was seen carrying groceries from a store for a distance of about a mile within a week after bearing a child.

Because of the strong desire for children birth is one of the major events in the life of a Manzaneño. This event is not merely biological in nature for it also functions to promote interrelations among the families, making them one compact body. Because of these functions child birth calls forth a series of appropriate ceremonies.

As soon as possible the infant is taken to the church by newly-appointed godparents for baptism. There it is inducted into the church which is later to become one of the important controlling and guiding factors in its life. The choice of godparents is of supreme importance for they have in addition to religious duties the function of looking out for the best interest of the godchild. In the event of trouble the Manzaneño feels free to go to his godparents for help. Thus, by this custom many of the Manzano families are even more closely integrated.

After baptism ceremonies continue. I attended such a ritual given in a house near the Quarai Pueblo ruins. The parents were living in one room of this house belonging to a friend. Initially the godparents attended morning mass at the Manzano church and afterwards brought the infant to the church to be baptized and then took it at noon to the parents. The grandparents then gave the name "Maria Concepción" to the baby. Usually this custom is overlooked, however, if the parents have a special name for the child. The children generally are given a name taken from the Bible.

Soon after godparents enter the house the godmother says a long special prayer. In the event the godparents do not know this prayer it is said by anyone familiar with the words. The parents or whoever know

the answer respond, "Recibe esta rosa amada que de la iglesia salites

con los santos y el agua que recibites" ["Receive this loved rose for

you came out of the church with the saints sanctified by the water you

received"]. The madrina [godmother] replied, "Recibe esta rosa amada que

de la iglesia salio con los santos sacramentos en el agua recibio" [Take

this loved rose for you came out of the church sanctified by the saints

with the water that you received"].

After the prayer, cookies, candy and liquor were given to the

guests. Then followed a dinner, first served to the guests. The menu was

meat cooked with rice; a chile stew of potatoes, meat, chile and beans;

coffee, canned pineapple and bread. Biscochitos, a type of cookie, were

also served. The balance of the ceremony consisted in drinking, eating

and singing accompanied with a guitar and accordion. The ritual

concluded about three o'clock in the afternoon.

Compared to many Anglo-American children, the Manzano children are

as a rule well-behaved, rarely crying or causing trouble. I rarely

observed a parent spanking his children. Babies are placed in the care

of their older brothers and sisters, who watch and guard them as closely

as their parents do. As soon as the girls are able physically they are

expected to help with the housework while the boys help in the fields.

Young girls also do their share of weeding and hoeing the fields. The

godparents spend many hours with the children, talking and singing to

them. The parents take pride in their children, showing them off to

their guests. If they can afford it a string of coral beads is bought

for the children.

Obedience and respect for parents and elders is taken for granted

and, according to one informant, all elders in the village had the right to give orders to the younger people and children whether they were related or not. If the children disobeyed the elders their fathers whipped them. This custom, no longer prevalent, may have had its origin in the peon-patrón in which absolute obedience was required of the servile group to the master. Rarely do young men smoke or curse in their father's presence.

Customs Relating to Food and Food Preparation

One of the main functions of the woman in the home is the preparation of food. This occupation fills a great amount of her time since she must cook on a woodstove, fireplace or outdoor oven. In the techniques of food preparation the influence of the American Indians is evident. Some women use the mano and metate to grind corn and use a gourd dipper for mixing water with food. Strips of melons and squash are hung outside on lines to dry for future use. Some women still prefer Indian-made pots for storing water and cooking beans. Tortillas are often cooked on flat stones, Indian fashion. On the whole, however, the Manzaneños have adopted the American table ware and cooking utensils.

Corn and beans gathered from the fields are often supplemented by fruits and greens that grow wild in the area. The crops include chokecherries, gooseberries, lamb's quarters, cow's tongues and pinons, all of which are considered delicacies. The Manzaneño still prefers his native recipes which have a mixed Spanish and Indian origin.

A common food, adobo, is made from long, thin strips of pork (tasojos). After the meat is sliced it is placed in a tub of boiling water containing chile, oregano (a wild and a cultivated herb) and sometimes garlic. Then it is hung on a line to dry. It is warmed in a pan placed in an oven before it is eaten. Another indigenous food is galletos, consisting of biscuits made of medium ground whole wheat [semitas] mixed with beef.

Menus of typical meals that I ate in Manzano homes show a limited variety of dishes. In a meal I was served at Lucas Zamora's house there was coffee, raw milk, pinto beans, green chile sauce, homemade goat cheese, tortillas and fried potatoes. In a meal at David Candelaria's house there were tortillas, green chile, raw milk, syrup and coffee with cream and sugar. The homemade goat cheese of the first meal was covered with molasses and eaten as dessert. The food was cooked in modern utensils and napkins accompanied the food. It is noticeable that all the food was home grown and home prepared with exception of the coffee and sugar.

Hospitality to strangers is characteristic of Manzaneños. A person entering one of the houses, especially one belonging to an old man, is treated as an honored guest even though it may be his first visit. He is offered the best seat in the home and if he does not seat himself the host is noticeably annoyed. Children, especially if they are very young, are placed in another room where they usually remain for the duration of the visit. The guest is nearly always served something, perhaps only a cup of coffee but usually tortillas, biscuits, cookies, beans and chile are proffered. This custom is observed at any time of day and it is improper for the guest to refuse. Furthermore, it is customary for the host to invite the guest to remain for dinner. During the meal host and guests are seated at the table first and the women serve. As the guest departs the host says "llequan" [come back].

Customs Related to Health and Sickness

Matters of health and sickness are usually taken care of by the family for as yet, private physicians are not consulted except in the event of extreme sickness. Births are usually attended by the local midwife, Pablita Romero. There are several reasons for this such as the lack of money for medical care, faith in native remedies and religion and the peoples' conservative nature. Furthermore, the nearest physician lives in Mountainair, some eight miles away and often inaccessible during the winter months because of snow and in the summer, mud. Many of the local medicinal practices may be categorized as superstitions. For example, their belief that sickness is caused sometimes by brujas [witches] reinforces the reliance on local curative practices (Hurt 1940A). Thus, thin slices of potatoes are placed on the head to cure headache. To draw out infections cigar stamps or strings of corn are placed on the wrists, forehead, neck or other afflicted parts. Gold is laid on the chest to draw out inflammation and strips of cigarette paper are placed on a wound to stop bleeding (the latter being an efficacious treatment). Skin shed by a snake is also placed on cuts to stop the flow of blood. A Manzano herb doctor reported that a Spanish-American man from Abó came to him to be treated for gangrene. This man had been using a poultice of manure for the problem (Hurt 1940A:193-201).

The following are some of the herbs used at Manzano for medicinal purposes: (1) the wild rose hips, damanians and wild mint are used for stomach trouble, (2) the wild gourd is used as a laxative. (3) locally-grown tobacco is used as an antiseptic (4) inmortal is given to the babies for colic and (9) green chile is used to treat sore gums. Additional herbs are given in Appendix XIX.

Few figures relating to the state of health of the Manzaneños exist. Of a group of 125 households that I studied 13 men and 18 women

reported that they were in bad health. Some of these people were very
ill and most had to remain in bed sometimes for many months. Elderly
people afflicted with arthritis were common and very noticeable. During
the severe winter of 1939 epidemics of influenza, colds and pneumonia
ravaged the village. Among the group of men who worked at the Quarai
Pueblo ruins sickness was given as the most common cause of absence.
Even younger men who appeared to be healthy were often sick.

On the whole the Manzaneños are uncooperative with such
preventative measures as quarantine. If someone is sick all the family
and many friends gather around and spend the entire day sympathizing,
praying and talking. No examples of effective isolation of the sick did
I see during the influenza epidemic of 1939. Outside toilets are left in
an unsanitary condition and individual drinking cups are rare.

Wild plants serve additional purposes. For example, wild gourds are
used to rid houses of insects. They are boiled in water and poured into
a pan; the odor drives away insects. Yucca [palomilla de amole] is used
for washing the hair and sometimes clothing, a custom derived from the
Southwestern Indians.

Death Customs

Death at Manzano is a family, community and religious affair. In
1939 I had the opportunity to witness a funeral ceremony. A woman had
died at night and all during the next day relatives and friends visited
the house trying to comfort the bereaved. That night the body was laid
out on a table surrounded by lighted candles and the relatives and
friends gathered to mourn and pray. This ceremony, una velan, lasted
nearly all night. The next morning, Sunday, these same people gathered
in the house to mourn and pray. While mass was being celebrated in the

church the gravediggers were excavating a trench in the east churchyard
while a large crowd of villagers stood around and talked. Late in the
afternoon the body, lying in a coffin covered with an army blanket, was
brought to the churchyard in a horse-drawn cart, followed by a large
procession of people in automobiles and wagons. After appropriate
rituals by the priest the body was buried. This ceremony was similar in
its major features to that of the Spanish-Americans throughout the
Southwest (Barker (1931:28) and Scott (1923:81-82).

It is customary to have the church ring a bell on the anniversary
of the death or during the main fiesta. Death is not always viewed
calmly at Manzano. For example, one afternoon I heard a shrill screaming
and shouting in the town and a woman dashed out of a house shouting that
someone had just died. This event caused considerable excitement and
commotion among the villagers. I also observed several times women at
Manzano scratching themselves until the bled when one of their relatives
died.

Families customarily celebrate a mass in honor of the dead members.
For example, one family gave a mass for their father who had been dead
for six months.

<u>Summary</u>

In summary, it is evident that customs associated with family life
and related institutions such as courtship, marriage, child birth, child
raising, death, type of houses and furnishing, type of food and food
preparation have changed very little under Anglo-American influence.
Orphans, unmarried children and older people without income are taken
care of by various family members. People live in the same types of
houses as their ancestors. Little improvement was evident in sanitary

features or utilization of physicians. Perhaps, the major change is
courtship where the selection of partners is made by the prospective
married couple themselves rather than by their parents. As the young
people acquire automobiles the custom of "dating" becomes common.
Changes are also noted in the types of food eaten as items such as
canned pineapples are purchased in the local stores, although the extent
to which this occurs is limited by the family's cash income.

CHAPTER VII

CONTEMPORARY COMMUNITY LIFE AND ACTIVITIES

Introduction

Community life at Manzano centers on several activities, both organized and informal. In the organized category are the Roman Catholic Church, the Manzano Land Grant Commission, the public school, the political parties, and the Water Commissioners while the informal group includes such activities as card games, family visiting and personal contact among the village inhabitants.

Religious Activities

A major, active organization in Manzano promoting cultural integration is the Roman Catholic Church, its most visible symbol being a building on the north side of the plaza (Figure VI). This is a small rectangular structure with a gray stuccoed exterior, a rusted tin roof, a bell tower and an interior typical of the small Spanish-American churches in the mountain villages. Surrounding on two sides and the front is the cemetery; to the south is the long, rambling tin-roofed convento (Figure VII) in which the resident priest, Father José Guatier, lives. The convento is in a poor state of repair, preserving an atmosphere of the past century. The reception room, for example, contains many ancient political advertisements and old railroad maps while the walls of the study are covered with many prints of old rotogravure cards of Spanish-Americans and Indians. The yards of the church and convento are unkept.

The patron saint of the church is Nuestra Señora de Dolores. Each year at the fiesta celebrating this saint the priest appoints two padrinos [godfathers] of the saints in each of the various parishes of this church (Figure XXI). For this privilege they pay $20.00 each although they have the right to refuse the appointment. On July 19 there is a mass celebrated for this patron saint of Manzano which costs each of the padrinos another $20.00. Prior the fiesta they have to replaster and decorate the church, then pay for the mass and musicians, expenses that total about $70.00. At the ceremonies a collection is taken to help the padrinos pay for these expenses but the amount collected is rarely enough to pay all the costs. The padrinos have the privilege of keeping statues of the saints in the home, returning them to the church only during the fiesta. Since the church at Manzano has a resident priest the statue of the patron saint must remain there throughout the year. In addition, at Christmas time a sponsor or padrino is appointed for the Santo Nino [The Christ Child].

The patron saint is believed by the villagers to have a function of protecting and looking out for the welfare of the community. In honor of the saint on June 19 a ceremony is held called una visita, a procession in which is carried on a litter a statue of Nuestra Señora de Dolores (Figures XXIII). Men are allowed to enter the parade, but usually do not, indicating that women more than men participate in the church's outward rituals. The statue of the patron saint and its platform is decorated with paper flowers. In the procession is a group of about 20 women and girls who sing hymns and pray as they go from house to house. At each house they stop for several minutes. When finished at Manzano the saint is carried to nearby villages such as Punta de Agua by their respective inhabitants. At the completion of the ceremony the statue is returned to the church at Manzano.

On September 15 and 16 a fiesta is held at Manzano in honor of the patron saint (Appendix III). This fiesta, beginning with a mass and ending with a dance, is more than a religious ritual for it also serves to bring people from surrounding villages, of furnishing an approved outlet for recreation and the freedom to become intoxicated. It also strengthens the bonds between the villagers as they participate together for common goals. In addition, it provides the opportunity for young people to meet and become better acquainted. Present at the fiesta also are groups of vendors selling religious items and other objects in stalls in the plaza.

No other saints are celebrated with a fiesta, although at one time it was the custom for men named Juan and women named Juana to give an appropriate ceremony on San Juan's day. The entire community once celebrated this day by having the previously described corrido del gallo, which terminated when a man was killed. In 1939, however, San Juan's Day was celebrated with a dance in the local dance hall. The men during the day did not stop working in the fields.

Nevertheless, many villagers still regard saint's days with deference. This fact is illustrated by stories and beliefs associated with San Ysidro Day, May 15. He is the patron saint of farmers. All the local farmers observe this day for there is a strong belief that if they work on this day disaster will strike them. It is related at Punta de Agua that a young man, scoffing at this belief, set out to plant his bean fields on San Ysidro Day even though his mother warned him not to do so. After sowing a few rows of beans he noticed a black cloud gathering over the Manzano Mountains followed by a heavy wind. Suddenly a terrible rain began to fall, flooding his field and drowning all his livestock. Since then the man has never worked on San Ysidro Day.

The Christmas and New Year's season is celebrated in much the same way as the Anglo-Americans with much house visiting, singing and drinking. On New Year's night a large free dance is given in the nearby village of Punta de Agua. On Kings Day, January 8, 1940, the well-known Spanish-American play Los Pastores was enacted in the school house at Manzano. This is a play depicting the Christmas story. It was planned to give the Spanish-American ceremony Los Posados on Christmas Eve but a snowstorm prohibited it since the ritual is held outdoors. In this ritual a group of children go from house to house imitating Mary and Joseph seeking shelter for the birth of the Christ Child.

One of the main traditional religious ceremonies is El Rosario held in the local church every afternoon in May and October. I visited the church one afternoon in May and observed about 30 women and children inside praying and "counting" their beads. It was noticeable that no men were present since as mentioned before men rarely participate in church services.

The church and saints are considered capable of helping people out of trouble. For example, in times of droughts or when a person is seriously ill a single individual or a group of people will invoke the aid of a saint. As payment for this succor a promise is made to carry the statue of the saint around the village a certain number of times. This activity is called una promesa.

Several religious activities are personal or family oriented; for example, many homes have plaster of paris figures of saints to which they pray. It is reported that one man who lives about nine miles northeast of the village has an _oratorio_, a small private chapel. The _velorio_ ceremony is also personal. According to informants if a person desires something to come true that has an important bearing on his life he makes a vow to God, to the cross or to some saint that if his wish is fulfilled he will perform the _velorio_.

I witnessed a _velorio_ given by an old woman on May 3, 1940, Santa Cruz Day. On this day every year she feels obliged to perform the ritual since her wish was fulfilled by the Holy Cross. In the event of sickness however, the date may be changed. One year this woman gave the ritual on September 15th because one of her relatives was sick on Santa Cruz Day.

The rite was performed in a large house in which lived three families, all relatives of the woman. In the west room was the altar especially constructed for Santa Cruz, the Holy Cross. For background a large piece of white cheesecloth was hung on a wall. The altar itself was topped by a cross over which hung a small wreath of flowers. On the wall hanging was a small embroidered cloth with a female figure on it. At various places on the altar and the cloth hanging were tinsel and Christmas tree decorations such as glass balls, crepe paper frills and paper balls. On the wall to the south of the altar was a crucifix and a religious painting. The altar itself was made of five boxes of graduated size, one on top of the other, in effect a stepped pyramid. Embroidered napkins were placed on the altar top and on the steps were ten candles, two to each terrace. The Holy Cross on top was decorated in elaborately embroidered vestments such as a dress and flowers. In this ceremony Santa Cruz is considered to be the mother of Christ.

In front of the altar along three sides of the room benches were placed for the participants and guests. The relatives began arriving in the room about seven o'clock. The ritual of the _velorio_ began about seven-thirty with the singing of hymns, prayers and counting of the beads. The women, who were the more active of the participants in the early part of the service, knelt while the men retired to the back of the room and talked. About nine o'clock the part of the ceremony known as _el rosario_ began and the men joined in with the women, remaining however, in a side room where they knelt in deepest reverence.

El rosario began with a long prayer with the woman chanting "Sagrado corazon de nuestra Jesús" [Sacred heart of our Jesus]. The other participants answered the same. Afterwards a hymn was sung with the men joining in. A man who owned the _oratorio_ in the village of La Cienega, kneeling to the west of the altar, took the cross down from the top of the altar and placed in on the next lower step. The service continued with taking the cross downward one step at a time until it finally reached the floor. The ceremony ended with more hymns and prayers. As the cross rested on each step hymns were sung and prayers were said.

After a brief recess everyone rested. Then one by one they went on their knees to the altar and kissed the cross held by the godfather and godmother. During this part an old woman read a long prayer written on a piece of paper. In the end the godfather, godmother and this old woman bent over the cross and kissed it. Then there were more prayers and hymns. Everyone adjourned to a side room where coffee and cookies were served. After eating the participants returned to the altar to sing and recite prayers for the remainder of the night.

Some aspects of the religious life at Manzano are divided among the Roman Catholic Church and the community. For example, the priest buries the dead in the church graveyard [_campo_ _santo_] if the relatives are able to pay. Otherwise the relatives bury their dead in the communal burial ground, the cemetario, which lies on a hill to the northwest of the town overlooking the road to Capillo Peak (Figure IX). West of the limestone-walled graveyard is a large new white cross indicating the religious aspect of this graveyard. Graves are of several types: (1) those marked by white wooden crosses, (2) those marked with sandstone or limestone rocks with the names carved on them, (3) those marked by a bare stone and (4) those surrounded by a picket fence or a chicken-coop-like wood structure. None of the graves are marked by commercially-made tombstones. This graveyard on the whole has an unkept appearance.

A traditional custom is to place stone piles, descansos [resting places], along the route where the pallbearers rested in carrying the coffin to the graveyard. Stone piles are also placed along the roads and highways at the sites where people have met accidental death. These Spanish-American customs are widespread in the Southwestern states.

Local stories are told about the Catholic saints. For example I asked an informant, Antonio Gonzales, why a wood statue of San Juan in the possession of Eugenio Gonzales holds a skull in his hand. He stated that his father told him that when San Juan was young he always was getting into fights. One time his head was cut off by another man. San Juan's father prayed to God to give San Juan a new head. He finally got a new one and now holds the first skull in his hand. Antonio stated he does not believe the legend.

Although the Roman Catholic Church is still influential in the life of the Manzaneños there are signs that it is losing its former hold. More and more participation in the church is limited to women and children. Furthermore, several families refuse to go to church at all. Frequent comments that I have heard express dissatisfaction with the fees for such services as baptism, marriage and death. According to one informant the fees are as follows: $1.00 for baptism, $10.00 for marriage if the priest is given three weeks' notice and $14.00 if given less notice. Several of the men also expressed strong dislike for the resident priest.

Economic Activities

Sources of livelihood at Manzano include: agriculture, stock raising, work on federal relief projects, direct support from federal and state agencies, private employment and woodhauling.

A study of 125 households was made to find the sources of their income. The information came from interviews and files of the New Mexico Department of Public Welfare and the Works Projects Administration in Estancia. In the files of the latter agency there is the possibility that the amount of income stated was minimized since to qualify the applicant could not have more than a prescribed maximum income.

These households were supported as follows: (1) 53 households had aid from the New Mexico Department of Public Welfare which included 2 receiving Aid to the Blind, 29 receiving commodities, 20 receiving old age pensions and 2 receiving pensions because their husbands were in the penitentiary, (2) 6 households supported by having sons in the Civilian Conservation Corps, 22 households supported by the Works Projects Administration, (3) 1 supported by school teaching and (4) 23 households supported by agriculture and stock raising, 2 by woodhauling and 1 by miscellaneous part-time employment. These figures indicate that 119 household heads were employed leaving 7 without visible means of support. Fifty-three households, 53%, received direct aid from the New Mexico Department of Public Welfare, 29, 23.2%, worked on state and

federal projects and 37, 29.6%, were supported by private employment.
Thus, 80.4% Manzano households were supported by relief work or relief
agencies. In percentage of people on relief Manzano is greater than many
other Spanish-American villages of New Mexico.

According to Walter, Jr.,

> "Sixty percent of the Spanish-speaking villagers were forced to go
> on relief. In many communities every family was listed on the
> rolls. Federal relief projects have become the greatest source of
> income for the entire section of the population." (1939:3)

The employment figures for Manzano in 1938 are radically different
from those obtained from the files of the Works Projects Administration,
Estancia, for the years prior to 1938. These figures are given below in
Table IV.

TABLE IV

EMPLOYMENT AT MANZANO PRIOR TO 1938

Type of Employment   Number of Examples

1.	Farmer	52
2.	Sheepherder	17
3.	W.P.A. worker*	24
4.	Railroad	1
5.	Miner	2
6.	Schoolteacher	2
7.	Freighter	3
8.	Construction (Conchas Dam)	1
9.	Carpenter	2
10.	Sawmill worker	8
11.	Farm laborer	2
12.	Road work	1
13.	Conservancy laborer	1
14.	Foundry worker	1
15.	County assessor	1
16.	Blacksmith	1
	Total	116

*Does not include those on other forms of relief for which
no figures were present in the W.P.A. files.

A comparison of the types of employment prior to 1938 and in 1939
shows an almost complete reversal in frequencies, even though the Great

Depression had existed for six years when the former figures were obtained, a fact indicating the progressive loss of private employment at Manzano vs. a shift to dependency upon Federal relief programs. Thus, prior to 1939, 24 plus another estimated 9 households or 28.4% were supported by relief programs vs. 82, 71.6%, by non-relief programs. Noteworthy was the decrease by almost two-thirds of the people supported by agriculture and stockraising, that is 69 prior to 1938 vs. 23 in 1938.

Vital to the economy of Manzano is the communal water system controlled by the Water Commissioners. The allocation system determined by the mayordomos [commissioners] arose in Spanish-American culture many years before Manzano was founded and is typical of many other Spanish-American communities of New Mexico. At Manzano this system came into being, apparently, when the first community dam was built in the first decades of the last century.

The water has its direct source in the large spring, the Ojo del Gigante, located near the southwest side of the village. Indirectly the water comes from the rain and snow, seeping into the ground, that falls in the Manzano Mountains to the west. Thus, most of the water that flows in the stream is directly proportional to the amount of moisture falling in the mountains. The highest flow from the spring on record was 3,129 acre feet in 1916 according to the Docket of Water Facilities Administration, Soil Conservation Service, Albuquerque. During the extremely wet spring of 1939 I estimate that enough water flowed for over 4,200 acre feet based upon a comparison of rainfall for 1916 and 1939.

The water in this limestone sinkhole, approximately 50 feet deep, is permanently flowing; even during a year of drought such as 1938 it produced a large amount of water. From the sinkhole the water flows out by an underground passage and reappears at another spring about an eighth of a mile to the east. There the water is stored behind a small cement dam. From this dam it flows in a meandering stream into the large artificial reservoir on the south side of the town (Figure X). Until 1939 the dam of this reservoir, constructed during the last century, was built of rock and crib work. This older reservoir was estimated to have held enough water to cover four acres a foot deep.

The old dam on the north side of the village was washed out about 45 years ago. In the area of this reservoir are now growing several small orchards. The basin here could still be used to store water, at least during the wetter years. For example, a large amount of water flowed in the spring time up to the middle of May in 1939 and would have filled the old reservoir area.

The allocation of water at Manzano was and still is administered by a _mayordomo_ and three commissioners, who are elected on the first Tuesday of December every other year. Although the elections are usually held it is a common occurrence for the same individuals to hold office over a long period. For many years the exact functions of the water commissioners were not clearly defined. The commission elected on December 2, 1918, adopted a series of rules and regulations (Appendix II). The Water Commission exercises the right to exact labor from members of the community at certain times of the year for maintenance of the ditches and the reservoir. It is possible that this system of communal labor was adopted from the Pueblo Indians (United States Department of Agriculture 1935B:79-89).

Before the advent of the present Water Facilities Administration there were about 1,000 acres being irrigated at Manzano. Since this was far less than could have been irrigated by the amount of water available

a movement was started to improve the situation. A promise of

cooperation was given by the Soil Conservation Service and the Farm

Security Administration to the Manzano Land Grant Commissioners. As a

result, the Commissioners held a meeting and posted this announcement

explaining in detail the initial agreement with these agencies. This

announcement stated as [translated into English]:

> "Probably it is known by all the heirs of the Manzano Grant that
> very soon will begin the project of development of the spring at
> Manzano. This work is to be done in cooperation with the federal
> agencies of the S. C. S. and the F. S. A. that represent the
> government in this work with 'water facilities' or is the work of
> conservation and development of water.

> "In this project the government will furnish all the materials and
> supervision of the work and the people of the Manzano Grant will
> furnish the common labor and teams as their contribution. Nobody
> will have to pay anything other than the government which will
> spend about $14,000 in materials, transportation, heavy machinery
> and technical help.

> "As this project will benefit directly or indirectly all the heirs
> of the grant and all those who have an intention of using the
> water, we issue an invitation not only to the owners of the fields
> and those who use the water regularly, but to all the heirs of the
> grant to help in their part of work to complete this project of
> which we are proud.

> "The apportionment of the work will be according to the benefit
> that a person derives from the water. It is figured for the
> duration of the project the heirs that do not use the water
> regularly are to donate a day's work a month; and the owners will
> be assessed in proportion to the amount of their irrigated land.

> "We hope for the good cooperation of all the heirs of our grant to
> make more valuable our property."

>   "Commission of the Manzano Grant
>   Anastacio Candelaria
>   Santiago Silva
>   Patrosinio Giron"

As a result a meeting of the villagers was held and they all agreed

to start repairing the spring and building a new community dam (Figure

XIX). According to a docket of the Water Facilities Administration,

Albuquerque,

"All of the individuals contacted in regard to this plan expressed their willingness to cooperate and showed their enthusiasm for the proposed work. Not a single operator was found to be opposed to the project and even the owners of the smallest units agreed to cooperate within their means."

This alleged cooperation was not apparent to me since I found many individuals dissatisfied with the proposal. For example, several people held to the belief that the dam was not to be built for the benefit of Manzano but to furnish a water supply for Mountainair. Others objected to the plan of everybody having to furnish labor without pay. Some suggested that the proposal had been "railroaded" through so that the Water Commissioners and Grant Commissioners would have a paying job. As the dam was being built complaints continued to be frequent. Workers from Punta de Agua required to furnish labor often commented that they could see no reason for working at Manzano for nothing since they would receive no actual benefit of the impounded water supply. A Manzaneño accused the Water Facilities Administration of impracticality, stating the this agency started building the ditches at their drainage end rather than at the place where they joined the dam. Because of this it was necessary to let the water in the tanque [reservoir] go to waste for several months during the farming season. If the ditches had been constructed first by the dam the water could have been utilized as the ditches progressed in length. In spite of the criticism and unwilling workers at Manzano the dam was finally built.

When construction began on the new dam the old one of rock rubble was torn out and a large earth fill structure was laid in its place. An elaborate system of concrete spillways and iron water gates was constructed while the old ditches were all rebuilt. A new aqueduct was built to conduct water to the south side of town.

According to the Water Facilities Administration the ditches when finished extend for about four miles and can irrigate approximately 2,437 acres, depending upon the water supply at any one time. The irrigable acreage is divided into 72 separate tracts or units with 45 owners and 47 operators. To administer the project a new mayordomo and water commissioners were elected at a special meeting held in Manzano on January 8, 1939. By the beginning of March, 1940, the water had completely filled the reservoir. The following year water began to seep out of the dam through underground passages, provoking the Manzaneños to continue to criticize the project.

Whether the leak was repaired is unknown to me since I concluded the investigation while the dam was still leaking. Later agreements reached between the federal agencies and the Manzaneños concerning the dam were: (1) the dam will remain in the hands of the government for five years, (2) the maximum land that any one person can irrigate is five acres, which will be prorated according to the total amount of land that a person owns and (3) if the water in the reservoir runs low everybody will be given a day's turn, or less, to irrigate and no more than the mayordomo designates.

The Water Facilities Administration made an investigation of the 47 households with irrigable land and disclosed the following: (1) the total amount of irrigable land owned by the households amounted to 909.65 acres with an additional 552.95 acres rented, (2) these households also owned 1,836.2 acres of non-irrigable land averaging 43 acres, (3) only 784.5 acres of the non-irrigable land were cultivated, averaging 18 acres per household, (4) the 47 households investigated averaged 4 individuals per unit and ranged from 1 to 11 acres in size and (5) 27, or a little more than half of these households were or had been supported by the Works Projects Administration, 2 by the Farm Security Administration, 1 by the Civilian Conservation Corps and 6 by the New Mexico Department of Public Welfare during the two years preceding the investigation. In summary, half of the households that owned irrigable land were at least partially supported by public relief programs. The fact that the average acreage owned by people with irrigable land is nearly twice as high as the average of the 125 households that I investigated indicates that the former group probably had a higher average economic status and scale of living.

The files of the Works Projects Administration at Estancia contain information on the private indebtedness, that is debts not owed to federal and state agencies, of 51 households at Manzano. Total private indebtedness of these households was $8,895.71, averaging $175.71 and ranging from none to $689.00. Only three households were free of debts.

In common with other Spanish-American communities of New Mexico Manzano has five grant commissioners controlling the communal lands. When the first land grant was made in 1829 by the Mexican government each of the village heirs received 80 acres. As land was continued to be allotted to heads of households the number of acres was reduced to 40. Although the Manzaneños still may petition for land there is very little remaining unallocated. Nearly all that is left lies in the rocky hill country between Manzano and La Cienega and has little economic value. A man must be 21 years old to petition for land; however, orphans, through adults, may petition for land at any age. The heir has the right to sell his land at any age. Titles in the Manzano Land Grant are recognized by the United States Government which patented the land in 1908 (Keleher, 1929).

That land which is held in common by the community may be used by all residents for cutting timber, grazing and rock hauling. The land is controlled by five Land Grant Commissioners elected every two years. Like the Water Commissioners the grant officers tend to retain their positions over long periods of time. The treasurer and the president of the board receive $1.50 for each grant petition they handle. The commissioners hold the right to sell the timber rights on the communal land or to sell the land itself. The money from such sales goes into the grant's treasury and is used for transportation of commissioners, hiring of lawyers, etc.

In 1939 there were 610 heirs or title owners in the Manzano Grant. Fifteen of these heirs acquired their land during the term of office of the present Grant Commissioners. Because of the large and increasing number of heirs the land grant parcels that they inherited are becoming smaller. This is caused mainly by the Spanish-American custom of dividing up the land among all the heirs rather than giving it to only one son or one daughter.

An investigation that I made of 125 households indicated that the average amount of land owned by each unit was 24.1 acres. This is larger than the amount owned by some of the other Spanish-American communities in New Mexico. In Taos County Spanish-Americans own, according to Sanchez, 2,200 acres, half of which are only six acres or less (1940:62). In the Cuba Valley, New Mexico, 80% of the Spanish-Americans own less than 25 acres (United States Department of Agriculture, 1937A:52) while at Manzano only half of the households own less than 25 (United States Department of Agriculture, 1937C:5). At Manzano 7 of the households rented 224 acres of land which averaged 32 acres per household.

The table below shows the size of the farms at Manzano of the 125 households that I investigated:

TABLE V
SIZE OF FARMS AT MANZANO

Number of Acres	Number of Households
100 or more...........................12	
75 – 99................................9	
50 – 74...............................15	
25 – 49...............................25	
2 – 24...............................16	
1.....................................8	
less than 1..........................40	
total..125	

Since much of the land is rocky and otherwise unsuitable for cultivation many families do not have sufficient land to support themselves by agriculture. The Docket of the Water Facilities Administration, Albuquerque, confirms this observation. It states that there is only one place as large as 185 acres and only a few men own from 25 to 50 acres (actually 51 men).

According to the U. S. Census of 1930 (Agriculture, I:419) the people of Manzano cultivated only 3,600 acres of the 7,683 owned; 148 acres were left idle or fallow; 2,013 were plowable but had never been plowed; 1,018 were woodland and all other uncultivated land amounted to 788 acres. All other land in farm was 175 acres. In 1930, 40 acres had crop failures which indicates that for this year at least the drought was very severe. Several reasons explain why more land was not plowed for much is rocky and needed for pasture.

The 1930 U. S. Census also showed the total value of farm lands and buildings to be $127,920; all farm buildings, $13,330; farm dwellings, $12,330 and implements and machinery, $14,000. This places a value of $16.64 per acre.

Table VI below from the Tax Assessor's Office shows the following valuation placed on property in Manzano Precinct:

TABLE VI
TAX VALUATION OF PROPERTY IN THE MANZANO PRECINCT, 1938

```
Land value.................................................$17,577.00
Improvements.............................................. ..3,859.00
Tangible personal property.................................1,345.00
Farm, ranch products and equipment.........................1,380.00
Equipment supplies............................................40.00
Merchandise, fixtures and equipment value...................835.00
Assessor's gross valuation................................31,381.00
Exemptions, family........................................13,729.00
Ex-soldiers' exemption.....................................1,348.00
Final value subject to taxation...........................16,304.00
Total valuation in 1939...................................30,873.00
```

Since this was an evaluation for tax purposes the valuation of the land and buildings in 1930 of $127,920 in relation to the $17,677 for 1938 it does not necessarily indicate a decrease in value since property is assessed for tax purposes less than its market value.

Agriculture at Manzano is of two types, dry farming and irrigation. Forty-eight farmers out of an estimated 100 have land that can be irrigated. With the addition of the improved water supply resulting from the construction of the new reservoir about 1,000 acres can be irrigated. The irrigated crops include sweet corn, peas, beans, greens, squash, tomatoes, cauliflower, cucumbers, asparagus, carrots, beets, onions and cabbage. In addition, forage crops such as alfalfa and clover are irrigated as is a small amount of native tobacco, punche mexicana, for local consumption. This tobacco is very strong and only a few old men smoke it. Common crops which are dry farmed include corn, oats, winter wheat, sorghums and beans. The yellow and white varieties of corn are most common but blue corn is grown and preferred for making tortillas and atole. Red corn is grown for chicken feed. For a cash crop,

surplus beans and corn are sold. Thus, the Manzaneños are partially
dependent upon dry farming. The fields only yield in a good year about
15 bushels of corn and 150 pounds of beans per acre. According to the
Soil Conservation Service improved farming techniques and conditions
should yield 25 bushels of corn, 600 pounds of beans and two tons of
alfalfa per acre. The soil is clay loam and fairly fertile provided
there is sufficient moisture. Also recommended is the planting of more
winter wheat and alfalfa.

Only three farmers of the area have many fruit trees. In the
entire Torrance County in 1919 3,835 bushels of apples were harvested,
representing a gain over the 3,500 harvested in 1909. By 1929 the number
had declined to 2,320 bushels (United States Department of Commerce
1910, 1920, 1930). At present nearly all the fruit trees are raised on
the east slope of the Manzano Mountains. The Water Facilities
Administration estimates that there are not more than a hundred fruit
trees on irrigated land in Manzano. The two large apple orchards in town
are the property of the local church. According to Bailey, the Manzano
region, providing sufficient water can be obtained for irrigation, is
suitable for growing fruit because of its high altitude, about 6,800
feet, which prevents most fruit trees from blooming too early and being
nipped by frost (1913:70). Apple, pears, plums and cherry trees do best
while peach and apricot are not well adapted because their blooms are
killed during the late frost. In spite of the suitability for growing
fruit trees and the long history of the two apple orchards the
Manzaneños have not taken advantage of this opportunity probably because
they prefer to raise beans and corn on the irrigated land rather than
fruit.

The Manzaneño is naturally faced with the same problems of the Anglo-American farmers of the Estancia Valley and his cash income is highly correlated with that of the latter group of people. Because of the varying amount of rainfall crop failures seem characteristic of the area as a whole. There were three complete crop failures during the 15 years previous to 1937 in the Tijeras Canyon Area to the north. Only a few farmers made a crop in 1937. In 1938 there were many examples of complete crop failure while in 1939 the number was lower. In 1940 and 1941 large crops were made by most farmers. At Manzano, however, while there may have been crop failure during these years on the dry farmed land the fact that the local spring furnishes permanently water for irrigated land would indicate that there was not complete crop failure. Weed and insect pests are also prevalent while variations in the price of beans and the demands of the market place often work hardship on all the Estancia Valley farmers. In addition, competition with the more efficient Anglo-American farmers increases the burden of farming at Manzano.

Concentration on bean raising has lessened the importance of other crops grown in the Estancia Valley. Most significant of these secondary crops are corn, wheat, sorghums, hay and cereals such as rye and oats. Recently the Farm Security Administration has attempted to induce farmers to raise crops other than beans, the plan being to curb the overproduction of beans and thus raise prices. During the years from 1927-1937 the price of 100 pounds of beans has varied from $1.25 to $4.75 (United States Department of Agriculture 1937C:35).

During the harvesting season in the Estancia valley only a few laborers from Manzano are hired for the bean crop. They are paid low wages, averaging one dollar and one meal for 10 to 12 hours of work. In the Moriarity region Indians from the Rio Grande Valley are preferred since they work harder than the Spanish-Americans. For the same reason the carrot farmers near Estancia hire Filipinos and Navajos. During the planting and cultivating season some outside laborers are hired by the Anglo-American farmers but generally they use family members for this purpose. Thus, these practices prevent the Manzaneños from supplementing their incomes by working as hired farm laborers.

Many of the agricultural practices have a very wide distribution among traditionally oriented farmers. Proper times for planting and plowing are determined by a series of natural omens. For example, the older farmers plant their corn when the oak leaves come out from their buds. Closely correlated with this custom are the methods for predicting weather, the majority of which are signs of bad weather. A sure sign of bad weather, it is said, is the occurrence of a small rainbow in the west at sunset. This kind of rainbow is called the ojo del buey [ox eye] by the Spanish-Americans and "sun dog" by rural Anglo-Americans of New Mexico and Texas. Related to this phenomenon is a circle around the sun and moon, called cerca del sol [fence of the sun] and cerca de la luna [fence of the moon] also supposed to indicate bad weather. Other signs of bad weather are horses running fast in herds, flies becoming sticky and particularly obnoxious, red sunrise with mackerel clouds, sheep gathering close together, birds flying hurriedly in large flocks towards the mountains and ants disappearing into their holes. Another method of predicting the weather at Manzano is to observe the phase of the moon. When the corners or "horns" are up there will be good weather; when the corners are down, bad weather.

The older Manzaneños say that the weather for the year can be predicted by the cabanuelas [ruling days], a belief also held by some of the rural Anglo-Americans of New Mexico and Oklahoma. According to this belief the type of weather for the first 12 days of January determines the weather for the twelve months of the year in sequence. The days from the 13th to the 24th of January determine the weather for each month in reverse order. The six days from the 25th to the 30th also determine the weather for the year but in this order: the morning of the 25th determines the weather of January, that of the afternoon of the 25th determines February, the morning of the 26th determines that of March and so forth. The weather of each of the 12 daylight hours on the 31st of January also determines the weather of the year in their natural sequence. To make a final prediction for the weather for each month of the year it is necessary to take the average of each group of ruling days.

During the month of April the Manzaneños generally plow their land with a walking plow drawn by a team of horses. They must plow early to prevent weeds from growing and drying out the soil. The planting season, however, varies with the times and amounts of rainfall. During 1938 corn and beans were planted from April 26 to the early part of May while in 1939 the crops were planted much later because there was a long dry season during the last part of spring and early summer. Nearly all the crops dry farmed failed in 1938.

Most farmers at Manzano have horses; none owns a tractor. Several, however, rent mechanized equipment. Farming implements are usually limited to a walking plow, a hand-made sled with a lateral knife for weed cutting, a lister, planter and cultivator. Only a few farmers have all this equipment. To overcome this lack they frequently rent, share or exchange equipment. Some Manzaneños rent threshing machines from Anglo-American farmers. For this equipment they must pay 15 pounds of beans per 100 and furnish labor and expenses. Some farmers still thresh beans by having horses trample the dried plants.

The Manzaneños, mainly because of the cultivation of the former grazing land in the Estancia Valley for agriculture, no longer have sufficient pastures for large herds of goats, sheep or other kinds of livestock. The decline of amount of grazing land was caused by the entrance of homesteaders in the first decade of this century. This was much later than the decline of the range cattle industry of New Mexico as a whole, which has been estimated to have occurred about 1855 (Willoughby 1933:90). In 1930 there were still 974,904 acres of grassland and 68,837 acres of woodland being used as pasture in the Estancia Valley (United States Department of Commerce 1930:312).

The Tax Assessor's Office at Estancia lists for 1938 and 1939 the following value and amount of livestock in the Manzano Precinct:

TABLE VII

NUMBER AND VALUE OF LIVESTOCK IN THE MANZANO PRECINCT

Type	1938	1939	Value in 1938
Horses	164	140	$4,289.00
Cows	66	73	1,309.00
Pigs	5	0	30.00
Sheep	168	79	530.00
Goats	0	133	0.00

The above figures for tax purposes appear to be underestimated for a survey of 125 households in Manzano in 1939 showed (1) 182 horses, (2) 60 cows, (3) 33 pigs, (4) 147 goats and (5) 587 chickens. The figures for the amount of sheep were accidentally lost. These figures indicate that there was only one cow for every two households, one and a half horses for each, one pig for every three, four and a half chickens for each and less than one goat for each household. These averages are deceptive, however, for all the horses are owned by 74 households, all the goats by 1 man, all the sheep by 3, all the pigs by 23 and all the chickens by 43 households. Thus, a large number of households own no livestock. The largest number of horses owned by one household was 8; the largest number of chickens, 36; cows, 5 and pigs, 2. Thus in spite of the unequal distribution of the livestock no one household owned a large number of livestock if comparison was made in the past century when some of the patrones are reported to have had hundreds of livestock. The fact that only 74 households of 125 own horses explains the difficulty that many Manzaneños have in farming. Only one man today has two burros, which was the traditional animal used for hauling wood.

Sheep raising still employs several Manzaneños during the spring. The largest herds in the region are owned by people outside of Manzano and are grazed in the Manzano Mountains, in the higher elevations with juniper and pinon forests and in the eastern part of the Estancia Valley. The lambing season begins about April 20 and lasts for 15 to 20 days. At this time a considerable amount of help is required to cut the sheep into small flocks and to protect them from the coyotes. For the entire period the sheepherders receive from $20.00 to $30.00 and food. It is reported that herders may still obtain sheep by the partido system from a store owner in Mountainair. I found, however, no record of a Manzaneño taking advantage of this opportunity.

Most of the horses in Torrance County are of the inferior class locally called "Indian ponies". They run in weight from 700 to 1,000 pounds, are badly nourished and seldom sell for more than $50.00. Rarely are attempts made to improve the stock by selective breeding techniques, a factor contributing to the inefficiency of farming.

The large herds of cattle in the county belong on the whole to Anglo-American ranchers for the Spanish-Americans own only a few head. It is noteworthy that during the first 15 years of homesteading the number of cattle increased despite the shrinking of grazing land. Since then the number and value of cattle have declined (United States Department of Commerce, Agriculture 1930:335). Recently attempts have been made by the government to stimulate the cattle industry by farmers to raise winter wheat for forage but whether this was successful is unknown.

Goats form a supplementary class of livestock raised in the county. In 1930 the U. S. Department of Commerce showed only 1,867 of these animals. At Manzano only one family derives a major portion of its income from raising goats. Other types of livestock raised in the county include swine, mules, turkeys and chickens. With the exception of chickens these other types of livestock contribute only a small amount to the county's income.

Several federal agencies aid the farmers of Manzano as well as those of the entire Estancia Valley. For several years the Soil Conservation Service in cooperation with the Civilian Conservation Corps maintained a camp in Red Canyon, a short distance southwest of Manzano. In addition to the financial help given to the families of Manzano who had a son in the program the Manzaneños benefited by contour furrowing on the farms of the region and the construction of dikes and other forms of erosion control. Some of the Manzano farmers refused, however, to permit this work on their lands. I asked one farmer what he thought of the government building contour dikes on his land and he replied that he had no use for such structures for weeds grew on them and it took all his time trying to get rid of the weeds. Another farmer objected to contour plowing his land, stating it was too hard to do this type of plowing.

The Farm Security Administration office in Estancia lends money to the Manzaneños for seed and other farm expenses. Some of the officials admitted to me that they had little expectation of ever getting the money back. In a group of 47 households that I surveyed three owed the Farm Security Administration $3,519.00, averaging $1,173. The heads of these households admitted that they had no intention of paying back the loans, although it is not known whether they had sufficient financial resources to clear the debts. The inability of Spanish-American farmers in many sections of New Mexico to pay back government loans has been noted in government reports (United States Department of Agriculture 1937C:5).

The Soil Conservation Service has proposed three methods to improve agriculture at Manzano (United States Department of Agriculture 1937C). They are

"1. Development of the water supply system, which will provide a more adequate water supply to irrigate every farm unit under the plan. Many crop failures have been occasioned in the past by erratic water supply, and as a consequence, farming has been a hazardous project.

"2. Initiation of an educational program among the farmers with emphasis on improved cultural and cropping practices, designed to increase production, improve the quality of farm products, and add to the subsistence income of each farmer.

"3. Demonstration to the farm families of methods for preservation of farm products by canning, drying, and storing. This is an important phase of the program, as few people in this community have knowledge and equipment for this work and it will contribute materially toward making them more self-sufficient."

To further such a program the dam at Manzano will remain in the hands of the government for five years. It is estimated that 90 families will benefit directly by the project and others by increased economic status in the village. Further programs recommended by the Soil

Conservation Service are increasing the number of fruit trees, planting winter wheat and rotation of crops using alfalfa and grasses such as broom corn, red top, blue grass, timothy and clover. The dam was constructed but the success of the other programs was not investigated because my survey was terminated soon after the proposals were made.

To overcome a land shortage some of the Manzano farmers endeavor to rent acreage. This is done on a share-crop basis, usually one-third to one-fourth for the use of the land. The relative lack of farm tenancy at Manzano has been observed among Spanish-American communities throughout New Mexico (Walter, Jr. 1938:53).

Income from private employment, other than farm labor, is uncommon at Manzano. Occasionally employed are two carpenters, three blacksmiths and two woodhaulers. Full-time employment is confined to one local school teacher, the Tabet family who operate one store and a bar and the Candelaria family which operates a general store. Records of the Tax Assessor's Office in Estancia indicate that in 1939 Tabet's store had $625 in stock and a building worth $300 and Candelaria's store had a stock value of $225 and a building worth $100. Tabet's store is the larger of the two and does the most business. Tabet states that most of his business is done on a cash basis because of the difficulty of collecting bills. Produce is not often taken in as trade on bills.

The lumber industry no longer furnishes employment for many Manzaneños. During 1938 and 1939 I did not find any villagers engaged in this type of work, undoubtedly caused by several events. There is only one small lumber company now working in the Manzano Mountains that is not only facing a shrinking market but also a decreasing supply of timber because of the incorporation of much land into the Cibola National Forest and the exhaustion of trees on private land. The present use of trucks at this small mill threw out of work the former teamsters from Manzano.

On several occasions some of the people of Manzano have had employment in the lime kiln near the graveyard. When the new schoolhouse was built this lime industry was temporarily revived. Near the large spring is the ruins of an older lime kiln.

Relief Workers Attitudes Toward Work

With the advent of the Roosevelt Administration, the "New Deal" agencies such as the Works Projects Administration and the Civilian Conservation Corps became a major source for employment of the men at Manzano. Because of the low standard of living and cash income of the Manzaneños a large number of them applied for relief and were given help at one time or the other. Of the 125 households investigated in 1939 17% of the heads were employed by the Works Projects Administration and 19% had been formerly employed. This makes a total of 36% who were or had been supported by the Works Projects Administration.

As a result of employment on relief programs there have been major changes not only in the economic life of the Manzaneños but also in their attitudes toward work. There is no evidence that the new income is used to buy land, livestock or equipment to increase their ability to make a living. Instead, they make purchases that they would not have made in the past such as buying automobiles valued at $50 to $100, with little thought of how they can pay for them. As a result many of the cars are repossessed in a short time. Nevertheless, the new cash income makes possible their ability to buy small items such as sewing machines and radios, for which they are able to pay.

Another major effect of the relief work is that it has enabled the Manzaneños to travel more. According to local informants trips to Albuquerque, Santa Fe and Belen are more frequent than in the past. Local informants also state that the employees on relief projects are slow to pay their debts even though they receive a steady cash income. The owners of grocery stores, general stores, and automobile dealers complain of the difficulty of collecting debts from the workers of the Works Projects Administration.

The tendency toward remaining on relief when once qualified was evident in the years 1938 and 1939. In this period of two years among a group of men from Manzano and Punta de Agua employed by the Works Projects Administration at the Quarai Pueblo Ruins only one man resigned to accept private employment and he was from Mountainair. In addition, few of these men voluntarily applied for loans from the Farm Security Administration, according to the administrators of this program. The personnel of this program stated that the Manzaneños have to be taken off the relief rolls and forced to apply for a loan. Only one man at Manzano did I hear say he was glad to get back to farming when he was laid off the Works Projects Administration and given a farm loan. A major factor in this preference for relief work was the uncertainties of local farming as opposed to a steady income from working with the federal agencies. Nevertheless, this kind of work is building up a dependency upon welfare programs rather than upon self-sufficiency.

While working as laborers on the Works Projects Administration project at Quarai the Manzaneños rarely strive for better positions. For example, when the position of stone mason opened up only two men applied for it. After this position was filled it was found that there were several men on the project who were more skilled stone masons than the men who applied for the position. Since the position of stone mason paid a greater salary that of the common laborers it appears that many of the Manzaneños do not value a salary much greater than that needed to satisfy their basic needs. If the average Manzaneño can earn a salary of about $50.00 a month he seems satisfied.

The attitude is well reflected in the Manzaneño regarding relief work as a necessary evil. While many prefer to work for the Works Projects Administration to farming, they regarded government employment as something to slide through as easily as possible. This attitude was expressed by a truck driver on the Quarai Project who was being scolded by a foreman for procrastination at his work. He replied, "Why should you worry? The government is paying me not you." A deception practiced on relief projects is to post a guard to warn the approach of a foreman when a work gang is loafing on the job.

Working for the Works Projects Administration has not made the employee take any pride in his work. On the Quarai project men from Manzano classified as skilled masons were content to build walls that repeatedly had to be torn down to pass government inspection. An outsider was admiring a small museum building that had been constructed in a period of about two months. The visitor stated that he would like to have a house built like the museum but he would hate to pay the cost of two months' construction. One of the laborers answered, "Oh, we can build you a home in a short time for practically nothing; we built this house for the Works Projects Administration."

This lackadaisical attitude toward work can not be attributed solely to the philosophy of the Manzaneños. The purpose of the Works Projects Administration was to provide emergency income to people suffering from the Great Depression and the droughts of the 1930s rather than promote efficient construction projects. This objective stood in marked contrast to employment by private contractors, who emphasized efficiency. In addition, a large section of the American people viewed the work done by employees of the Work Projects Administration as a boondoggle. The Manzaneños recognized this and consequently did little more than a minimum amount of labor. In spite of the low status of relief work many of the Manzaneños ignored cards sent to them by the employment offices in Estancia offering the opportunity of private employment.

Most serious for the Manzaneños was the growing dependency upon relief work to make a living, an attitude reinforced by the first time having a steady income vs. the uncertain success of farming or the necessity of working harder for private employers. The most serious result of this dependency was the abandoning of fields by some of the farmers who obtained relief work. During the year 1938 several farmers at Chato, an outlying settlement of Manzano abandoned their fields and offered to rent them for an exceedingly small fee. In the years 1938-1939 I observed many fields by Manzano lying unused or only partially cultivated while their owners drew government pay.

The attitude of dependency, other than working for short periods in the sheep camps, for employment by public relief programs is further borne out by the fact that while the Manzaneños and the people of the nearby community, Punta de Agua, look to the government for income not many of them are willing to aid or help the program with its problems. For example, an employee who had worked for a year with the Works Projects Administration was laid off the Quarai project because he had obtained private employment. When the foreman of this project asked the man for a donation of a few stones from his land the latter refused, demanding payment instead. Another example is the following: the Quarai project was filling in an arroyo with debris from the excavation of the Indian ruins. This arroyo was seriously cutting away the land of the owner and the debris would have checked it. Nevertheless, the owner of the land made the project stop the work saying if he wanted to stop the arroyo from eroding away his land he would fill it in himself. He also said he could see no reason for letting the government save a long haul to dispose of the excavation debris. At Quarai the water from a small stream was diverted to fill in an old bed of a pond to make the area more attractive. Since the small amount of water from this spring was not utilized by the farmers down stream for irrigation it was thought that there would be no objection to the plan. Nevertheless, the foreman of the project was ordered by local people to stop diverting the spring water because, "Damming it would interfere with Punta de Agua water system!". The water was not utilized by the inhabitants once the dam was taken out.

Some of the antagonism expressed by the Manzaneños and the people of their neighboring communities may be a reaction to the racial discrimination from which they suffer in their relations to the local Anglo-Americans. Torrance County is almost evenly divided between English and Spanish-speaking peoples. According to the New Mexico State Planning Board, 49% of the inhabitants spoke Spanish and 51% English (1935:40). The local Anglo-Americans do not view the Spanish-Americans as social equals. So strong is this prejudice that an Anglo-American loses status when he or she marries a Spanish-American. This prejudice is borne out in the work place, in schools, in the bars and dance halls where there are gang fights between the two ethnic groups.

A long working day does not make much difference to the Manzaneños.
for many of the laborers rise at four o'clock in the morning and work
until sunset. Yet they do not hesitate to gather into groups, stop
working and talk, often for long periods of time. Their attitude may be
summed up in these words, "Why not work long hours and enjoy yourself
while working instead of working hard for a short period of time and
then trying to entertain yourself during leisure time?" This attitude
was observed by Walter, Jr. in other Spanish American communities of New
Mexico. He states,

> "Although the Spanish-American people shun unusual efforts, it is
> a mistaken notion that laziness is characteristic of them. They go
> about their labors in an unhurried manner, but they do hard
> manual labor for hours. For the physically able, the work day
> lasts from before dawn until after dark; they perform their tasks
> cheerfully and do better at group tasks than at individual
> occupations". (1939:53)

The Anglo-American concept of time and hurry appears to be foreign
to Manzaneños. For example, it is difficult to find villagers willing
to commit themselves to a definite time when they will start some
enterprise. Although it is largely a myth, the Anglo-Americans consider
the Spanish-Americans to have a "mañana" attitude or wait until tomorrow
to do something.

The common accusations by Anglo-Americans that the Spanish-
Americans are an impractical people does not apply to all Manzaneños. I
was commenting on one occasion to an old man about the beautiful scenery
around Manzano. The man replied, "Yes, the country is pretty but it is
so dry that we can barely raise a crop on it." The practicality of some
of the villagers is borne out by the fact that they accept old clothes
willingly and remake them into suitable garments.

Most people at Manzano do not look forward to the future with
either serious or pleasurable thought. It may be said that it is the

past and the present, not the future, in which the Manzaneños live. Many of the Manzaneños, in particular the older ones, look upon the past with longing. It was in the old days, they say, not the present, when everybody had work and sufficient food. In this observation there is more than a grain of truth. There is also a definite desire among some of the older people to change things back to past conditions. Several people look forward to the world coming to a disastrous end, with the more religious ones quoting passages from the Bible and the more practical ones pointing to the present world-wide economic depression.

The School

The Manzano public school is another focal point of community activity. The first county-supported school was started about 1905 in a building across from Tabet's store. Prior to the establishment of the county itself there had been private schools which were supported by the communities and the individual households. Informants state that the duration of the term in these private schools depended upon the amount of money the community gave. Usually these schools were held in private homes, lasting only in the winter months with the number of teachers varying from one to three. Most individuals, however, received what little education they had from the family and from the Roman Catholic Church in catechism and singing classes.

The public school at Manzano opened with about 60 pupils and two teachers. The problems of the latter were lessened materially by the director's prompt action in appointing a third teacher. The location of this first school is not known to me. Several years later another public schoolhouse was built. Informants state that it was a stone building with four rooms. In 1935 the building was destroyed by fire. In

1938 laborers of the Works Projects Administration built a new school, a well-made building with four rooms made of stone and two of adobe (Figure V). Two homemade basketball courts form an important part of the scanty athletic equipment.

In 1939 there were five teachers at the school teaching the primary and the eight grades. Only one of the teachers is a resident of Manzano. The others are Spanish--Americans and Syrians living in nearby settlements. Salaries of these teachers average $720.00 a year and are lower than the average of $901.59 for all the rural school teachers of New Mexico (Brown 1929:54). The table below lists the teachers in 1937 and the other staff members.

TABLE VIII

SALARIES OF MANZANO SCHOOL TEACHERS AND STAFF, 1938*

Name	Position	Salaries per month	Residence
José Salas	principal	$88.50	Manzano
Elene G. Gurule	teacher	82.00	Manzano
Mary Tabet	teacher	82.00	Mountainair
Lola Tabet	teacher	82.00	Mountainair
Crucita Otero	teacher	82.00	Willard
E. Sanchez	bus driver	80.00	Manzano
Juanita Turrieta	janitor	18.00	Manzano
Canlo Buol	maintenance	20.00	Manzano
Eduardo Gonzales	maintenance	20.00	Manzano

*Information from Torrance County Superintendent of Schools,1938

Length of the school term varies. In 1939 it began on August 28 and ended in April, a term of seven and a half months in contrast with New Mexico's four room schools of eight months. The principal stated that eight months was the longest the school could stay in session because the children were needed to work in the fields. While school is in session, however, no free time is given for harvesting or other outside work.

School teachers complain that the parents of pupils are not cooperative, that they generally lack interest in the school and that they rarely visit the classes. An example of the lack of cooperation, one teacher stated, happened during one of the school plays. On that occasion there were not enough chairs and none of the townspeople offered to bring any. Furthermore, the local merchants could not be induced to furnish kerosene lamps. The Manzaneños, however, do not withhold their children from school nor do they object to them learning English.

The Manzano school has witnessed an increasing number of pupils until 1937 and then a decline while number of teachers remained the same after 1936-37 as indicated in the table below.

TABLE IX

NUMBER OF PUPILS AND TEACHERS AT MANZANO

Year	Number of pupils	Year	Number of teachers
1933............64		1918-19.........1	
1934...........103		1919-20.........2	
1935...........100		1920-21.........1	
1936...........160		1921-34.........*	
1937...........121		1935-36.........3	
1938...........114		1936-37.........5	
1939...........132		1937-38.........5	
*figures missing			

Table X below indicates that the age and grade distribution of the children in the Manzano school is similar to that of Belen, a mixed Anglo-American Spanish-American town in the Rio Grande Valley. (Tolle 1929:54). This table also shows that the majority of the pupils in the Manzano school drop out after the fifth grade. The explanation given for the drop-outs is that the children are needed to work in the fields or that they are too poor to go to school since they cannot afford to buy appropriate clothing. Several male informants, however, told me they dropped out of school because they were tired of it. The table also shows that in the primer the sexes were almost evenly divided, that more males attended the higher grades but that more women completed grades six and seven. The latter figure may result because more men were needed for field work but as previously mentioned several men stated that they were bored with school and dropped out.

TABLE   X

GRADE, SEX, AND AGE DISTRIBUTION OF MANZANO PUPILS, NOVEMBER, 1939

Grade	Males	Females	Total	Age Range
Primer	21	20	41	5 – 9
First	7	7	14	7 – 9
Second	12	5	17	7 – 11
Third	13	9	22	8 – 15
Fourth	2	3	5	11 – 13
Fifth	10	6	16	11 – 16
Sixth	3	5	8	11 – 14
Seventh	1	3	4	12 – 13
Eighth	2	3	5	13 – 16
Totals	71	61	131	

The only high school available to Manzano children is the one in Mountainair, a small town eight miles to the southeast. Since only a few students have finished the eighth grade in the Manzano school not many students have been eligible to attend high school in Mountainair. In addition, the road from Manzano to Mountainair is frequently impassable due to heavy snow during the winter and mud during the summer. Nevertheless, the principal of the Manzano school stated that all the students who graduated from the Manzano school in 1939 went to high school in Mountainair. I do not, however, have a figure for the number of students who graduated from the Manzano School in 1939 but it was probably not more than 5 (the number who were in the eighth grade in 1939), if that many. The 100% attendance of high school by the Manzano school graduates in 1938 ranks far above that of 366 American cities surveyed by Ayers (Tolle, 1929:74). In these cities it was found that only 71.4% of the eighth grade graduates entered high school. I was able to find only one native of Manzano who had attended college and this individual did not obtain a degree.

Table X shows the attendance of pupils at the Manzano School, 1938. The approximate 90% attendance at Manzano ranks far above the average attendance of 75% in all the four room schools in New Mexico and 78% of the city schools.

TABLE XI

ATTENDANCE OF PUPILS AT MANZANO SCHOOL IN 1938

Grade	Days missed	Possible total days
Primer	94	700
First and Second	*	*
Third and Fourth	39	494
Fifth and Sixth	27	353
Seventh and Eighth	27.5	260
Totals	187.5	1,867

* Figures missing

One of the problems faced at Manzano is the difficulty of transporting children to school. While a large number of the children can walk to school, the remainder live in nearby rural areas and must use the school bus. The difficulty of walking to school during the winter months at Manzano is revealed in the figures of Table X that show the younger children miss more school days than the older. In 1939 forty-nine of the pupils rode two buses to school, while three more came on bicycles. Buses are not an ideal solution to school attendance since they lengthen the pupil's day and add to the expense of the already impoverished school. According to Brown yearly cost per pupil for school buses in Torrance County is $69.61, the highest rate in New Mexico (1929:11).

The Manzano school board has three members, Max Sedillo, Semion Herrera and a Mr. Sena. They are elected for a three year term that is so arranged that one of them resigns each year and a new member is elected. Election practices are lax; for example, in 1938, there was no election, the old members remaining. The board is nearly functionless, according to the principal. Because of politics they have little influence nor do they often meet to discuss policies. Recommendations by the board are usually ignored by the County Office of Education. The school sponsors a minimum of outside activities since the main recreation of the children are informal games such as marbles, tops and sand lot baseball. The older male students state that they prefer to play basketball. The principal tried in 1938 to establish a 4-H club but was unsuccessful. The school organized a basketball team but was handicapped by the lack of funds to buy athletic equipment. In 1938, four Spanish-American plays were given by the school children for the general public, Los Pantalones, La Muella del Judío, and the traditional Christmas play, Los Pastores. To celebrate the Coronado Cuatro Centennial a play was written by the school staff and presented to the public. Attendance was crowded at all these plays, proving an exception to the general rule that the parents do not visit the school.

Literacy

Although the Manzano school appears to be making progress in the elimination of illiteracy in the village, the older people have not been affected. An investigation that I made of 120 individuals who were either married or 21 years of age is shown in Table XI. Eighteen men,

28.5%, and 14 women, 24.6%, had received no education. Average number of years of school for men was 3.45 years and for women, 3.31 years. Mode for both sexes was no education. The men ranged from 0 to the tenth grade and the women the same. The 53.1% illiteracy for the Manzaneños surveyed ranks far ahead of the 13.3% for New Mexico as a whole (Ackerman, 1933:51).

TABLE XII

AMOUNT OF EDUCATION OF ADULT MANZANEÑOS

Number of years	Number of males	females	Total
none	18	14	32
1	2	3	5
2	7	7	14
3	5	9	14
4	7	7	14
5	7	4	11
6	6	4	10
7	2	0	0
8	8	7	15
9	0	1	1
10	1	1	2
Total	63	57	120

Until 1936 there was a slow growth in the number of teachers as revealed in the following figures: 1918-1919, one teacher; 1919-1920, two teachers; 1920-1921, one teacher; 1934-1935, 3 teachers; 1935-1936, 4 teachers; 1936-1937, 5 teachers; 1937-1938, 5 teachers; and 1938-1939, 5 teachers.

Folklore, Superstitions and Folk Medicine

Because of illiteracy or very little education many of the adults of Manzano still believe in witchcraft, have many superstitions and use folk medicines. On the basis of interviews I arrived at the following classification of folklore at Manzano: (1) a belief in witches [brujas] and witchcraft, (2) belief in the mal ojo [evil eye], (3) religious superstitions, (4) buried treasure stories (5) farming superstitions, and (6) superstitions relating to the evil portent of certain activities such as breaking a mirror or a lamp chimney.

Older informants still remember a Tajique witch named Serafina who was reported to have been the owner of several figurines [monos] into which she stuck pins to bewitch people (Hurt 1940B:77). However, no one was able to find these monos. One time the sheriff, Dario Sanchez, took her to court for practicing witchcraft against a half-breed Indian at Manzano but he was unable to find enough evidence. Once Serafina and another witch named Petrona, formerly of Mexico, had a fight. Serafina threatened to turn her into a dog. Women in Manzano that had children were particularly afraid of the mal ojo. According to this belief if a woman stared at their children there was danger of their dying.

In a comparative study of superstitions and witchcraft of Manzano and Bernalillo, a town near Abuquerque, it was found that the inhabitants of the former village was less superstitious than the Spanish-Americans in the latter town (Hurt, 1940A, 1948B). Since Manzano is a relatively isolated mountain village and Bernalillo, a community located near a large city, we might expect the inhabitants of the latter town to be more skeptical of witchcraft and other superstitions. The attitude of the people of these two communities when telling a bruja story well illustrates the difference. Nearly all Manzano story tellers begin their tales with the following reservations: "My uncle (or some other person) told me this story when I was a boy (or girl)". There may have been witches a long time ago but I never seen one myself." Very few Manzaneños now admit that they still believe in witchcraft and witches.

In Bernalillo, on the other hand, the informants tell a witch story as if they were an actual witness to the event and take for granted that the listener also believes in these superstitions. The similarity of the superstitions and witch tales told at Manzano are closely related to those told by the Spanish-Americans throughout the Southwest, indicative of a common origin. Historical evidence seems to indicate that the basic characteristics were brought to the New World by the Spanish immigrants. In the Spanish-American villages of the central Rio Grande but not at Manzano some of the tales show a Pueblo Indian origin.

The use of native herbs for remedies against sickness abound. Max Zamora, a 65 year old informant, stated that the following are herbs useful for stomach trouble: oshá, mostrauso, yerba buena and cobo.

According to David and Manuel Candelaria the Manzaneños use these herbs:

1. yerba buena (peppermint) used for stomach aches by boiling it in water and drinking it. It is also used in wine making.

2. oshá, a root, is chewed for stomach trouble. This plant resembles the peppermint.

3. cachania for stomach distress and headache.

4. inmortal for pulmonary troubles; it is drunk hot or put on the chest.

5. canaigra, a root placed on the teeth for toothache.

6. punche mexicana, locally grown tobacco, is used as antiseptic for cuts.

Yerba buena grows naturally near the reservoir. Oshá and cachania are grown in the yard while the others are indigeous to the mountains.

If a person has the tis, a disease where his heart and gums are sore, it is claimed, he can cure it by eating green chile. One man tried to cure this disease by immersion in hot springs but he died. David Candelaria gets a pain twice a day in his legs followed by the pain going to his head. This problem has been going on for two years. He stops what he is doing and says, A Dios [Oh God] and the pain then goes away. Additional local remedies are shown in Appendix XIX.

Politics and Local Government

Local elected governmental officials include the School Board, the Land Grant Commissioners, the Water Commissioners, the Justice of Peace and the Constable with the rank of deputy sheriff, all serving for a two year term. In addition, there may be more than one deputy sheriff.

Partisan politics are taken seriously at Manzano, the subject forming a popular subject for conversation. Until the advent of the Roosevelt administration in 1932 with its "New Deal" relief programs, according to local informants, the local people voted 90% Republican. The shift toward the Democratic Party is revealed in the fact that of 366 registered voters in 1939 133 of the villagers gave their preference to this party. The County Clerk's Office in Estancia also reveals that 193 still preferred the Republican Party and the remaining 40 declined to state their affiliation. Undoubtedly the shift to the Democratic Party was a result of the local popularity of the "New Deal" relief programs.

The political leaders of the two parties in Manzano are the two storekeepers and their families. It is possible that this type of leadership is a hang-over from the days when the patrones controlled village politics. The strong dependence of Spanish Americans upon the jefe politico [political boss] has been noted by Walter, Jr. who states that, "In matters secular, economic, and political, the jefe politico is supreme. He is friend, guardian, and advisor." (1938:72)

In common with many other areas of New Mexico political scandals are frequent. For example, these events occurred during the county election of 1936, according to local informants and articles in the Estancia News Herald, February, 1936 to November, 1937. Frank Stephens, the Republican candidate, and James Albrinton, the Democrat candidate, were running for sheriff. Manzano was expected to vote Republican; consequently, the Democrats were very much worried. On election day the judges at Manzano became intoxicated, lost the keys to the ballot boxes and disarranged the books. Paul Tabet, the Democrat election judge, testified at a later date that on election day Pablo Lucero leading several men entered the ballot room, upset the ballot boxes and poured ink into them. The county judges did not show up that day and the local election judges did not try to count the ballots. Stephens knowing that Manzano had more Republican votes than Democratic took a pickup truck to Manzano to get the ballot boxes. For safety he took along an automobile procession. He was pelted with stones but not badly injured. In the main street one of the men who accompanied him, Eugenio Brito, was stabbed in the side and had to go to the hospital. Stephens delivered the ballot boxes to the County Clerk's office on November 4, beyond the 34 hour deadline prescribed by law. Stephens wanted the election judges to count the votes but Paul Tabet, the Democrat election judge, refused to participate in the counting saying that the ballots were illegal because they had ink on them. County Commissioner Garrison then tried without success to get the election judges to turn over the ballots. He then obtained a court order requiring the judges to deliver the ballots to him. The judges then gave the County Clerk the ballots. Because the deadline had passed the County Commissioners refused to count the Manzano vote and Albrinton was unofficially elected but could

not take office until the affair was straightened out. Meanwhile the
incumbent sheriff continued to hold office until January, 1937 when
Albrinton took his place. During this period the District Court ordered
the commissioners to count the Manzano vote but they refused. Finally
the case was taken to the New Mexico Supreme Court which ordered the
Manzano votes to be counted. The votes were then counted and Stephens
was declared elected as sheriff and he took office in the summer of
1937.

Another political scandal which involved Manzano occurred in 1937.
The Justices of Peace were up for election but the County Commissioners,
rather than permitting a vote to be taken, appointed them. At Manzano
Silviano LaJuenesse was appointed Justice of Peace and Blaine Brazfield
Constable. One election actually was held in Torreón but the
Commissioners declared this illegal. The District Court twice ordered
the Commissioners to take a vote but they refused. The case was finally
taken to the Supreme Court and they lost.

Other Community Activities

In comparison with the two nearby villages of Torreón and Punta de
Agua community activities at Manzano are relatively scarce. For example,
Torreón has a large community building in which are held many plays and
dances and a community workshop. Responsible for constructing the
building and sponsoring its activities are the Sociedad de San José and
the National Youth Administration. This religious lay organization is
only indirectly connected with the Roman Catholic Church, having its own
officers and managing its own finances. Its standard, however, is kept
in the local church. Other community activities in Torreón include the
celebration of San Juan's Day with a rodeo and chicken pull (corrido del

gallo). In the small village of Punta de Agua a tiroteo is given. This
is a contest to see which team of horses can pull the greatest weight.
None of these events are held at Manzano.

Dances   are   held   infrequently at Manzano. A baseball team was
organized in 1938 and appeared to interest the villagers. During Sunday
afternoon in late spring the team plays with those of the neighboring
villages. The bar and the two general stores form centers for meeting
people and gossiping. At the bar men gather for card games and drinking.
When not working the Manzaneños also spend a large amount of their time
on the porches talking. In this respect these activities are shared with
other Spanish-American communities. According to Walter, Jr., "Chief
recreation of the Spanish-American communities are embodied in the
fiesta and baile; various forms of gambling, drinking, intoxication,
liquors, visiting, and gossiping follow in close order" (1938:75).

Visiting between households is another type of community activity
at Manzano. During these visits usually all the members of a household,
including children, call on one another. Group singing, playing the
guitar and accordion are popular forms of entertainment in these visits.

In addition to furnishing a medium for sociability and recreation
music is the principal form of artistic expression. In comparison with
the Anglo-Americans musical activities are participated in to a greater
extent than among a typical group of Anglo-Americans; it is a rare
Manzaneño who can not play the accordion, the guitar or the harmonica.
Those who can afford it have radios; others with less means endeavor to
have a phonograph. Nearly all the villagers like to engage in group
singing, regardless of the quality of their voices. Women tend to sing
nasally, especially in church choirs. It is not an idle statement to say
that when the Manzaneño begins to sing he is expressing some of his

basic emotions and philosophy, that is, alternating feelings of deep sadness with mild happiness. Many of the songs are concerned with unhappy love affairs or events in their lives. Songs which recreate nostalgic visions of the past are common. Martial music and forceful, dramatic songs are absent. The difference in the preference for types of music between the young and the old is exemplified in their dances. Youths prefer dancing to "swing" music; elderly people to schottisches, polkas and waltzes. In comparison with the past the Manzaneños no longer compose original songs. Vanished are the regional troubadours such as Casimiro Lujan who wrote many ballads describing local events. Instead, popular Spanish-American music from northern New Mexico and music from Mexico are preferred.

Other forms of artistic expression such as weaving, pottery-making, wood carving and painting, which were once practiced at Manzano, are now forgotten. These products of local industries, which once served to make the people more self-sufficient have been replaced by purchasing manufactured objects from the traders.

On the whole the Manzaneños are friendly toward each other and toward strangers. While working they do not hesitate to stop and talk to each other for hours at a time. It is customary for older men to tip their hats when passing one another. Younger men usually tip their hats to elders but not to one another. The expression of friendliness includes the custom of waving to strangers who pass through the village in automobiles. It is also the custom at Manzano and in nearby towns to give aid and hospitality to strangers in trouble.

There are exceptions, however, to the general friendship and hospitable attitude of Manzaneños toward each other. One man while he was deputy sheriff incurred the disfavor of several of the villagers. He reports that he has been shot at several times from ambush while he was hauling wood and other supplies into the village. Recent construction of the community dam caused many quarrels among the Manzanenos. One dispute arose over whether or not to let outsiders swim in the reservoir. While some of the Manzaneños were in favor of this policy the Water Commissioners were not. As a result of this quarrel lasting enmities were created among some of the men. To avoid minor quarrels, it is the custom to draw matches to determine the winner.

Little effort is made by the community as a whole to improve the roads and the appearance of the village. Ruts and mud puddles are rarely filled in except through the efforts of the New Mexico Highway Department. In interviews that I had with the villagers direct questions to elicit their community pride were answered noncommittally or brought forth complaints about the unproductiveness of the region. One man did state, however, that he preferred Manzano to the Spanish-American villages in the Rio Grande Valley.

Summary

In reviewing the material presented in this chapter it is noticeable that many traditional community activities are in a process of abandonment. Dances, native games, folkways, arts and handicrafts are gradually disappearing. Community spirit, characteristic of the village in the past, is in a state of disruption. When the people of Manzano were asked by community leaders to donate their labor for improving the water supply many were uncooperative. The influence of the Roman Catholic Church is weakening and many men no longer attend church. Constant complaint is heard regarding the policies of this institution. Parents rarely visit the public school or assist in its activities.

Nevertheless, many old time customs such as elder men tipping their hats to each other continues. Attendance at the public school is high and Spanish-American festivals and plays are still given. Hospitality toward strangers is still a vital activity.

The greatest amount of change, however, is the shift from economic self-sufficiency to a dependency on income by employment on federal relief projects. For example, the records of the Water Facilities Administration show that 90% of the Manzaneños have received government and state relief. This lack of self-sufficiency can be attributed to the cumulative effects of the loss of grazing land for livestock raising, the shrinking of the lumber industry, the world-wide economic depression that began in 1929, an unusual number of serious droughts during the 1930s and the shrinking size of the family farm as the land is constantly divided among heirs.

To meet this problem several "New Deal" agencies have been applied to Manzano. Because of the relatively low income the average Manzaneño was able to qualify for aid. The success of these programs lies mainly in the fact that they have temporarily provided the households with cash incomes without which they could no longer survive. Unfortunately, evidence is accumulating that the relief programs at Manzano have instituted an attitude of dependency on them. The agricultural land that can be irrigated by the improved dam and reservoir is not fully utilized as some farmers prefer to work on relief projects rather than face the uncertainties of agriculture. The people tend to look upon these projects as permanent employment rather than look for private employment. Exceptional are the relief employees that quit to work in the sheep camps. The end result of the relief work programs is that the government, both federal and state, has become the new patrón. While the peon-patrón system in the past made for economic self-sufficiency the present government programs are having the opposite result.

Manzano has still retained its bad reputation for crime and political scandals. Whether the crime rate is as high as in the past was not determined. People in neighboring communities still express fear of going to dances at Manzano because of the frequent drunken brawls.

Of the many institutions at Manzano the public school appears to be the only institution that is becoming increasingly viable. That it has continued to grow in face of the local poverty, lack of equipment and lack of parental support is remarkable.

Manzano, as facts seem to indicate, is a community in a state of progressive disorganization. Whether this trend will change in the future remains to be seen.

CHAPTER VIII

SUMMARY AND CONCLUSIONS

In summarizing and drawing conclusions in this study of Manzano the cultural-historical method has been used. This technique has the advantage of presenting a continual picture of the community and is thus adaptable to the discovery of causal factors of the present-day conditions of the village culture. Methods used to elicit data included formal interviews with use of a schedule with local adults and outsiders knowledgeable about Manzano, informal interviews with local citizens and outsiders, participant observation, examination of files on Manzano in federal and government reports, and examination of relevant newspapers and books. In addition, I served as a supervisor of Works Projects laborers from Manzano and Punta de Agua. The descriptions of past conditions at Manzano is the part of this report most subject to error since it was largely obtained from elder informants who tend to see the past as a "Golden Age". It is doubtful, however, that this tendency of the older people at Manzano was any more exaggerated than those of elders in any society.

Throughout the history of Manzano, the peon-patrón system has been a major factor in the organization and integration of Manzano culture and society, although the individuals who were the patrones have changed through time. The first indication of its existence is found in the Land Grant Petition of Manzano of 1829, in which it was specified that

159

Colonel Bartolome Baca and Don Antonio José Otero were large landowners in the community. The full effects of the peon-patrón system, however, were not felt until some time later when Filimeno Sanchez and several other rich men entered the community and instigated the use of Indian slaves as well as indentured local citizens.

This institution was characterized by dependence of a large group of laborers, the peones and Indian slaves for nearly all their economic and other needs upon the rich landowners, the patrones, for food, shelter, clothing, health measures and to some extent advice on religion and on family and personal matters. It was possible for the patrones to assume control over free citizens and to maintain control of the peones by manipulating debts contracted by the individual or his parents. The son of a peon or Indian slave tended to remain, either by choice or by force, under the control of the patrón. This system, regardless of its negative features, was a major force in integrating Manzaneños into one compact body as well as reinforcing the preservation of the traditional cultural, economic, and social life.

After Manzano became part of the territory of the United States in 1848 and as a result of the consequences of the Civil War, the peon-patrón system as such became illegal. Nevertheless, this institution persisted with slight modifications other than the freedom given to the Indian slaves. Nearly all the peones and ex-slaves continued in service with the same patrón. The first real change came with the entrance of the Anglo-American lumber men, the Syrian traders, and the rise of the political chiefs, both local and outsiders. This represented shift in power as a whole to outsiders or to people born outside of the village. The end result was the loss to a certain extent of community independence.

Manzano remained under control of these new _patrones_ until the advent of the New Deal programs of the 1930s when the federal, state and county governments became the new _patrones_. Thus, the control of the community, almost completely passed to outsiders.

Basic to the economic system of Manzano is ownership of land for agriculture and livestock raising. The first inhabitants of Manzano acquired legal title to their land by the grant made by the Mexican government in 1829. At first the Manzaneños could petition for 80 acres of land but as more and more land was allocated, the amount was reduced to 40 acres. At present the remaining unallotted land is nearly worthless for economic gain. Originally, there was sufficient land to support each household. Through time, however, the villagers adhered to the Spanish custom of dividing the land equally among the heirs with the end result that the amount of acreage owned by each individual became progressively smaller.

During the nineteenth and the first decade of the twentieth centuries the basic source of livelihood at Manzano was livestock raising. Since this industry was capable of producing a cash income while agriculture served only for local subsistence it was of major interest to the _patrones_ who shipped livestock as far as California to provide food for the gold miners. There was available to the people for livestock raising the open range of the Estancia Valley where thousands of sheep and other animals could be grazed. In 1904 the Anglo-American homesteaders began arriving in the Estancia Valley and fencing the open range. With the gradual loss of land for grazing the number of livestock progressively decreased at Manzano.

Traditionally agriculture at Manzano was of secondary importance. Two types of farming were present, dry farming of corn and beans and

irrigating land for vegetables. Methods of agriculture were primitive
and utilized mainly human and animal labor. With the gradual shrinking
of importance of livestock raising agriculture became the predominant
economic base. For a cash income the Manzaneño farmers increased the
acreage devoted to pinto beans, taking advantage of the increasing
Anglo-American market for the crop. Nevertheless, the sale of beans has
provided an uncertain income because of poor prices, droughts, insect
pests and vagaries of the market place. Thus the cultivation of the
pinto beans was not an adequate economic substitute for livestock
raising.

An ill-defined but nevertheless a strong factor in integrating
Manzano society in the nineteenth century was the continual warfare with
the Navajo Indians, skirmishes that continued until the 1880s. For
defense the entire community was laid out as a large fort, vigilantes
were constantly prepared to fight and arms were always carried. In
addition, one of the large land owners and employers organized his
living quarters as a fortress with a watchtower. Involuntary labor in
maintaining the reservoir, dam and irrigation ditches was required of
all citizens and also contributed to community solidarity. The contact
with the Indians enriched the locals with items of material culture that
enabled them to survive better in their harsh habitat. Communally
organized buffalo hunts brought the villagers together for a common
purpose.

When the Anglo-Americans first entered the region, according to
Major Carleton, the Manzaneños maintained a hostile attitude. This
strong in-group vs. out-group feeling reached a climax in 1912 when some
of the Manzaneños and nearby Spanish-Americans built an arsenal at Abó
for the purpose of driving the Anglo-Americans out of the Estancia

Valley. Under the impact of the Anglo-Americans, however, many traditional aspects of Manzano culture began to crumble. The degree of acculturation with Anglo-American culture was far greater, both materially and non-materially, than that which occurred with Indian culture. This contact also left the Manzaneños with a confused and contradictory attitude toward the newcomers, for distrust, cooperativeness, uncooperativeness, antagonism and friendliness, naive acceptance of some cultural traits and rejection of others linked with feelings of despondency. Some individuals refused to cooperate or complained about the government efforts to improve their water supply, ditches and preventing erosion on their land. The Water Commissioners are met with refusals when they try to obtain help in maintaining the irrigation system. Parents do not often visit the public school. Mud holes and ruts in the town roads lie unfilled until they dry up or the New Mexico Highway Department sends in a repair crew.

Throughout the nineteenth century the Manzaneños were almost self-sufficient in their material culture, making their own pottery vessels, blankets, tools, farm equipment, etc. With the coming of the Syrian traders to Manzano many of these items formerly locally made were given up in favor of purchasing them. Nevertheless, this shift increased the need for a cash income. In this century also the locally produced poetry, music and ballads ceased as music of the Anglo-Americans and from Mexico were substituted. About the only artistic endeavors that still survive are the playing of musical instruments and group singing.

Manzano has long had the reputation for harboring criminals but whether it increased through time I could find no relevant data. Major Carleton stated in 1855 that this village had one of the worst reputations for moral degradation. Political scandals, robberies and assassinations have been characteristic. Neighboring villagers still are reluctant to attend Manzano dances because of drunken brawls.

Of the traditional institutions in Manzano the family and household organization is most intact. But even here a weakening is noted in that the parents no longer control the choice of marriage partners of their children. Still activities such as education at home, native medical lore, health practices, techniques of constructing houses and subsistence methods prevail. The sick relatives, the aged and orphans are taken care of by families. These changes in the family organization are beginning to be manifest, however as (1) education is being shifted to the public schools and (2) the federal and state governments are assuming more responsibility for the care of orphans, the aged, the poor and the sick.

The public school at Manzano appears to be the main local institution that is progressing in its mission since illiteracy is decreasing and more students are graduating from the eighth grade and entering high school. The influence of the school will undoubtedly cause local superstitions to disappear.

Final Conclusions

1. Manzano because of the adverse effects of the Great Depression, the droughts of the 1930s and the introduction of the public welfare programs is showing signs of community disorganization. Even prior to this the disappearance of the Penitentes and the traditional peon-patrón system and the weakening of the patriarchial family and the Roman Catholic Church may have actually initiated this trend. Other contributing factors were the loss of land for grazing livestock and shrinking of the lumber industry.

2. Nearly all the traditional arts and crafts have disappeared with participation in musical activities being an exception. Thus, Manzano has lost most of the richness of its culture.

3. With the loss of home industry and locally-made material culture the Manzaneños have become increasingly dependent upon a cash income to purchase their necessities in the local stores and in those outside of the village.

4. Organized community activities, dances, recreation and games are disappearing and now the people in Manzano in their leisure time engage mainly in visiting friends and relatives, gambling and drinking.

5. The Manzano School has progressed in decreasing illiteracy but as yet has not contributed to community solidarity.

6. Manzano has not yet lost its feelings of group solidarity since outsiders sometimes are victims of hostile attitudes.

7. Although the present programs of the federal and state government have contributed to the local cash income there is no evidence that they have aided community self-sufficiency and solidarity. Instead they have fostered an attitude of dependency. Nevertheless, without this aid the Manzaneños would have suffered extreme economic deprivation because of the Great Depression and the droughts during the last decade.

8. The decrease in population from 812 in 1940 to 424 in 1950 is a measure of the disintegration of the community, resulting from the progressive destruction of economic self-sufficiency.

9. A program aimed at rehabilitating the Manzaneños must include adult education programs. They need to learn how to better exploit their water supply for irrigated farming, to take advantage of the region's ability to produce fruit, and to improve their agricultural techniques.

Any suggestion that they return to the traditional economy which resulted in bare subsistence would not be acceptable to the people of Manzano. They have been subjected to much higher goals and expectations by the Anglo-American influence. With the need for a greater cash income to fulfill their present desires and expectations it can be questioned that Manzano has a sufficient land base to continue the traditional dependence upon agriculture and limited stock raising, Thus, migration away from the community by some of the younger generation seems inevitable.

10. Although economic changes brought about by stress of the Great Depression and the droughts of the 1930s have been emphasized as the major causes of the present state of community disorganization at Manzano the adverse effects upon the traditonal family and religious institutions resulting from Anglo-American acculturation must not be underestimated.

11. Since the major hypothesis of this report is that Manzano is in the early phases of community disorganization a follow-up study is needed to ascertain whether this is but a short-time trend.

REFERENCES CITED

Abel, Annie Heloise
    1915 The Official Correspondence of James Calhoun, While Indian
        Agent at Santa Fe and Superintendent of Indian Affairs in New
        Mexico. Government Printing Office, New York.

Ackerman, R. E.
    1933 Trends in Illiteracy in New Mexico. Unpublished Master's
        thesis. University of New Mexico, Albuquerque.

Anderson, George B.
    1907 History of New Mexico, Its Resources and Peoples, Vol.I.
        Pacific States Publishing Co, Los Angeles.

Austin, Mary
    1924 The Land of Journey's Ending. The Century Company, New York.

Bailey, Vernon
    1913 Life Zones and Crop Zones of New Mexico. North American Fauna
        No.35. Bureau of Biological Survey, United States Department of
        Agriculture, Washington D.C.

Barker, Ruth Laughlin
    1931 Caballeros. D. Appleton & Co., New York.

Bently, Harold W.
    1932 Dictionary Spanish Terms in English with Special Reference to
        American Southwest. Columbia University Press, New York.

Bloom, Lansing B., and Thomas C. Donnelly
    1933 New Mexico History and Civics. The University Press,
        Albuquerque.

Brown, Charles E.
    1929 Some Phases of Rural Education in New Mexico. Unpublished
        Master's thesis. University of New Mexico. Albuquerque.

Burgess, E. W.
    1925 The Growth of the City. University of Chicago Press,
        Chicago.

Carleton, James Henry
    1854 Diary of an Excursion to the Ruins Abo, Quarra, and Gran
        Quivira in New Mexico, under the Command of Major James Henry
        Carleton. Ninth Annual Report:296-316. Smithsonian Institution,
        Washington, D.C.

Chapin, Francis Stuart
    1935 Contemporary American Institutions: A Sociological Analysis.
    Harper and Brothers, New York.

Charles, Ralph
    1940 Development of the Partido System in the New Mexico Sheep
    Industry. Unpublished Master's thesis, University of New Mexico,
    Albuquerque.

Cuber, John F.
    1938 The Measurements and Significance of Institutional
    Organization. American Journal of Sociology 44:408-413.

Culin, Stewart
    1907 Games of the North American Indians. Twelfth Annual Report of
    the Bureau of American Ethnology. Smithsonian Institution,
    Washington, D.C.

Elliot, Mabel A., and Francis E. Merrill
    1941 Social Disorganization. Harper and Brothers, New York.

Espinosa, Aurelio M.
    1911 Penitentes. The Catholic Encyclopedia XI: 635-636.

Espinosa, Gilberto, and Tibio J. Chavez
    no date El Rio Abajo. Pampa Print Shop, No city given.

Ford, Karen Cowan
    1975 Las Yerbas de la Gente: A Study of Hispano-American Medicinal
    Plants.Anthropological Papers, Museum of Anthropology,
    University of Michigan, No.60. University of Michigan, Ann Arbor.

Greene, Charles W.
    1882 A Complete Business Directory of New Mexico and Gazetteer for
    the Territory for 1882. New Mexico Publishing and Printing
    Company.

Gringo and Greaser
    1883-1884 Newspaper published in Manzano. On file Museum of New
    Mexico, Santa Fe.

Harris, J. A., C. M. Jackson, et al.
    1930 The Measurement of Man. The University of Minnesota Press.

Hawley, Florence M.
    1936 Yes, We Have No Apples. New Mexico Magazine XIV[8]:16,17,433.

Henderson, Alice Corbin
    1937 Brothers of Light: The Penitentes of New Mexico.
    Harcourt Brace & Co., New York.

Hill, Willard William
    1937 Navajo Pottery Manufacture. The University of New Mexico
    Bulletin, Anthropological Series 2[3], Whole No.317.
    Albuquerque.

Hodge, Frederick Webb
    1907   Apache. Handbook of North American Indians. Bulletin 30
           Pt.2:63-67, William Frederick Hodge, editor. Bureau of American
           Ethnology, Smithsonian Institution, Washington, D.C.

Hurt, Wesley R.
    1939   Indian Influence at Manzano. El Palacio, XVI[5]:245-254.
    1940A Spanish-American Superstitions. El Palacio, XLVII[9];193-20.
    1940B Witchcraft in New Mexico. El Palacio, XLVIII[4]:73-82
    1941   Buffalo Hunting. New Mexico Magazine 19[11]:9,35,36.

Keleher, W. A.
    1939   Law of the New Mexico Land Grant. Reprinted. New Mexico
           Historical Association, Santa Fe. Originally published in New
           Mexico Historical Review IV.

Kluckhohn, Florence H.
    1940   The Participant-observer Technique in Small Communities.
           American Journal of Sociology XLVI[3]:331-343.

Kolb, J. H., and Edmund S. Brunner
    1940   A Study of Rural Society: Its Organization Changes. Houghton
           Mifflin Co., Boston.

Krodel, Gottfried George
    1968   Flagellation. Encyclopedia Britannica, Vol.9:410-411.

Lange, Charles H. and Carroll L. Riley
    1966   The Southwestern Journals of Adolph F. Bandelier 1880-1882.
           The University of New Mexico Press, Albuquerque, and the Museum
           of New Mexico Press, Santa Fe.
    1970   The Southwestern Journals of Adolph F. Bandelier 1883-1884.
           The University of New Mexico Press, Albuquerque.

Las Nuevas de Estancia
    1904. Newspaper published in Estancia.

Lasky, Robert S., and T. P. Wooton
    1933   The Metal Resources of New Mexico and Their Economic
           Features. New Mexico School of Mines Bulletin 7. Socorro.

Lynd, Robert S.
    1939   Knowledge for What. Princeton University Press, Princeton.

Lynd, Robert S., and Helen M. Lynd
    1929   Middletown. Hartcourt Brace and Co., New York.

Meinzer, O. R.
    1911   Geology and Water Supply. Paper 1. United States Geological
           Survey, Washington D.C.

Mindeleff, Cosmos
    1896   Aboriginal Remains in the Verde Valley. Thirteenth Annual
           Report of the Bureau of American Ethnology. Smithsonian
           Institution, Washington, D.C.

New Mexico State Planning Board
    1935 Second Progress Report. Santa Fe.

Park, Robert K., and Ernest W. Burgess
    1924   Introduction to the Science of Sociology. University of
    Chicago Press, Chicago.

Parsons, Elsie Worthington (Clews)
    1936 Mitla, Town of Souls, and Other Zapoteco-speaking Pueblos of
    Oaxaca, Mexico. The University of Chicago Press, Chicago.

Polk, R. L. & Co., and A. C. Danser
    1884 Colorado, New Mexico, Utah, Nevada, Wyoming, and Arizona
    Gazetteer and Business Directory, 1884-1885.

Reed, Erik
    1939   History of Quarai Special Report on Quarai State Monument,
    Ms on file National Park Service. Santa Fe.

Ripley, William Z.
    1889 The Races of Europe, D. Appleton and Co., New York.

Sanchez, George I.
    1940   Forgotten People. University Press. Albuquerque.

Scott, Florence Johnson
    1923   Customs and Superstitions among Texas Mexicans on the Rio
    Grande Border. Reprinted Texas Folk-lore Society. Originally
    published in Coffee in the Gourd. Texas Folk-lore Society.

Steiner, Jesse Frederick
    1928 The American Community in Action, Henry Holt & Co., New Work.

Sumner, William Graham
    1906 Folkways. Ginn and Co., Boston.

Tolle, Vernon G.
    1929 Report of the Belen, New Mexico School Survey. Unpublished
    Master's thesis. University of New Mexico, Albuquerque.

Twitchell, Ralph Emerson
    1914   The Spanish Archives of New Mexico, II. The Torch Press.
    Cedar Rapids.

United States Department of Agriculture
    1914   Docket of the Water Facilities Administration. Soil
    Conservation Service. Albuquerque.
    1935A   Preliminary Report on Concho. Regional Bulletin 29,
    Conservation Economics Series 2. Soil Conservation Service,
    Albuquerque.
    1935B Tewa Basin Study. Regional Bulletin 34, Conservation
    Economic Series 7. Soil Conservation Service, Albuquerque.
    1936C Reconnaissance Survey of Human Dependency on Resources in the
    Rio Grande Watershed. Regional Bulletin 33, Conservation
    Economic Series 6. Soil Conservation Service. Albuquerque.

1937A   A   Report   on   the   Cuba   Valley.Regional   Bulletin   36,
Conservation   Economic   Series   9.   Soil   Conservation   Service,
Albuquerque.
1937B Destruction of Villages at San Marcial. Regional Bulletin 33,
Conservation   Economic   Series   11.   Soil   Conservation   Service,
Albuquerque.
1937C   Tijeras   Canyon-Moriarity   Area.   Regional   Bulletin   39,
Conservation   Economic   Series   12,   Soil   Conservation   Service.
Albuquerque.
1937D   Preliminary   Report   on   Concho.   Regional   Bulletin   29.
Conservation   Economic   Series   2.   Soil   Conservation   Service.
Albuquerque.
1937E The Partido System, U. S. Forest Service. Albuquerque.
1940   Statistics   on Southwestern Region Arizona and   New   Mexico.
United States Forest Service. Albuquerque.

United States Department of Commerce
    1910   Agriculture.
    1920   Agriculture.
    1930   Agriculture.

Walter, Paul A. F.
    1916 The Cities that Died of Fear. Papers of the School of American
    Archaeology 35. Archaeological Institute of America, Santa Fe.

Walter, Jr. Paul Alfred Francis
    1933   The Press as Source of Social Problems. Unpublished Master's
    thesis, University of New Mexico. Albuquerque.
    1938   A Study of Isolation and Social Change in Three Spanish-
    speaking Villages of New Mexico. Unpublished Ph.D. dissertation.
    Stanford University, Palo Alto.
    1939   The   Spanish-speaking Community in New Mexico.Sociology and
    Social Research, XXIV:150-157.

White, Leslie A.
    1932 Historical Sketch of Acoma. Fourteenth Annual Report of the
    Bureau of American Ethnology: 23-193 Smithsonian Institution,
    Washington, D.C.

Willoughby, Roy
    1933 The Range Cattle Industry in New Mexico. Unpublished Master's
    thesis. University of New Mexico, Albuquerque.

Wirth, Louis
    1933 The Scope and Problems of the Community. Publications of the
    American Philosophical Society, Philadelphia.

Woodson, Charles W.
    1968 Peonage. Encyclopedia Britannica Vol.9:584.

Works Progress Administration
    1939   Inventory of the County Archives of Torrance County 29. The
    Historical Records Survey. Albuquerque.

THE MANZANO LAND GRANT PETITION*

"To The illustrious Corporation of Tomé

"Citizen José Manuel Truxillo for himself and in the name of the settlers of Manzano, whose names appear on the margin, with due respect to your Excellency, that not having deed of possession to the said town in which they have settled, and the site of said town being known to be owned by no one, we request Your Excellency to be pleased to grant us the possession thereof, giving us the land which we are now occupying, giving us as boundaries, from North to South, from Torreón to the old Mission of Abó, and from east to west from the tableland called Jumanos to the mountain, all of which is to be for pasture grounds and other common purposes, crops, roads, and other uses necessary for every town established upon all the solid basis of common and private property, and inhabited by the same, requesting further, as a condition for any of the above mentioned individuals or any others to be admitted in the future without injury to the former, to the new town of Manzano to acquire legal property therein, that he shall construct a regular terraced house of adobe, in the square where the Chapel is to be constructed (for which permission has been granted us) and he shall bring with him his property of every description, contribute to all community labor, procure the increase and prosperity of the town, defending with arms the firesides of the town to the fullest extent against any domestic or foreign enemy, and finally that person who will not reside in said town with the family belonging to him and who shall remove to another settlement shall lose all rights he may have acquired to his property. In view of all that has been stated we all and each of us request that your Excellency will be pleased through a committee of your body to establish the boundaries of the town at the points set forth, which being done, that we be compelled to establish proper monuments for the information of the settlers and the public within the entire Territory, granting us said land in the name of the Supreme Government of the Mexican Nation, to which government we belong, referring thereupon this our petition to the Most Excellent Territorial Deputation in order the proper approval may issue therefrom.

"Tomé. September, 22d, 1829.

To the Illustrious Corporation of Tomé

(Signed) José Manuel Truxillo"

"The Corporation of the Jurisdiction of Tomé in view of the foregoing petition, in session to-day, has resolved to refer said petition to the Most Excellent Territorial Deputation with the remark that this Corporation knows of no obstacle against granting to the petitioners the land they solicit, the only objection found being in regard to the arable land therein situated, belonging to Retired Lieutenant Colonel Bartolome Baca, who will be satisfied with the land which, as a new settler he may acquire together with that which he has purchased from other settlers, promising that, although he will not establish his residence there, he will cultivate and improve the lands which may be recognized as his."

"Tomé, September 25th, 1829.

(Signed) Jacinto Sanchez

(Signed) Juan Baca

Acting Secretary"

"Office of the Secretary of the Most Excellent Territorial Deputation of New Mexico.

"In the session of the 28th of November the last, this deputation resolved that the following Decree be added to the foregoing proceedings.

"By virtue of the foregoing report, the Corporation of Tomé the Justice of that jurisdiction will place the petitioners in possession of the land that they ask for, giving to each one the tillable land he may be able to cultivate, leaving the remainder for such other individuals who in the future may establish themselves therein limiting the boundaries to one league in each direction"

"(Signed) José Antonio Chavez,

President

(Signed) José Abrea,

Secretary."

"Manzano, December 24, 1829

"In compliance with the directions of the Most Excellent Territorial Deputation, as hereinbefore expressed, I proceed to this settlement of Manzano on the day of the date and all the inhabitants thereof being assembled I proceeded to give them possession of the aforesaid site in the name of the nation, establishing the center of said land the Alto del Pino de la Virgin, which is situated in the middle of the fields, the settlers having asked for that point and having measured their league in the direction of the four cardinal points of the compass as directed by the Most Excellent Deputation in their foregoing decree their boundaries were given to them as follows:

"On the north two solitary cedar trees in the Canyon del Alto, called the canyon of the deceased Ulas; on the West the summit of the hill which is on the western side of the Upper [torn out]; on the South the rise which is on the opposite side of the gully of Cienega; on the East, the Mesa Colorado, called the Rancho of Don Pedro de la Torre, and having placed them in possession, I proceeded to the head of the tillable land and having intimated to them that I was going to divide their lands by lot, in accordance to the foregoing decree, they unanimously answered, as requesting me to do the honor to let them retain the land they already improved, which request I deemed proper to comply with in order that no one should be dissatisfied.

"In Testimony whereof, I signed with my attending witnesses to which I certify.

"(Signed) Jacinto Sanchez

Attending

(Signed) Juan José Sanchez

(Signed) Merio Antonio Montoya"

Settlers of Manzano

José Manuel Truxillo
Diego Gonzales
Bernardino Chavez
Joaquin Sanchez
Antonio Torres
José Maria Marquez
José Antonio Torres
Juan Marquez
Mariano Torres
Gertrudis Benavides
Santos Marquez
Tomas Sanchez
José Cisneros
Ramon Cisneros
Estanislao Otero
Antonio Torres
Rayes Torres
José Leon Perea
José Manuel Garcia
Francisco Herrera

José Maria Perea
Juan Perea
José de Jesús Baldonado
Antonio Mirabal
Anastacio Mirabal
Juan Chavez
Juan Gonzales, Jr.
Juan Esteben Chaves
Faustin Sanchez
Francisco Velasquez
Juan Velasquez
Antonio Candelaria
Manuela Sena
Antonio José Garcia
Matias Montoya
Juan Archuleta
Juan de Herrera
Francisco Garcia
Nicolas Salazar
Matilde Montoya

Rafael Montoya

Ana Maria Barela

Jesús Savaadra

Juan Sedillo

Francisco Sedillo

Rafael Sedillo

José Sedillo

Juana Montoya

Alfonso Sedillo

José Mirabal

Diego Sanchez

José Dolores Jaramillo

Juan Castillo

Eulogio Saez

Miguel Chavez

Miguel Lucero

Nerio Montoya

José Maria Gonzales

Domingo Lucero

Francisco Torres

José Antonio Montoya

Juana Peralta

Guadalupe Perea

Amounting to 81

Further

José Sanchez

Pedro Chavez

Rafael Montoya

Eugenio Cordova

Julian Sanchez

Miguel Archuleta

Domingo Sanchez

Francisco Padilla

New Settlers

Pablo Gallegos

Alfonso Jaramillo

José de Jesus Maldonado

Nepomacino Luera

José Rafael Chavez

Juan Luera

Luis Romero

Manuel Salas

Francisco Sena

Marcos Sedillo

Juan Perea

Manuel Trujillo

Ignacio Sedillo

Pedro Sena

Jesús Sena

Trinidad Salas

Juan de Jesús Zamora

José Torres

Antonio José Otero

Manuel Chavez

José Sanchez y Cueva

Martin Gurule

Tiburcio Sanchez

Juan de Jesús Maldonado

Pablo Padilla

Candido Chavez

Manuel Sanchez Zamora

Juan Lucero

Francisco Romero y Luera

José Maria Torres

Francisco Romero y Campos

Juan Cruz Telles

Doroteo Salas

Miguel Chavez

Antonio Romero y Baca

José Padilla

Cruz Romero

Santiago Otero

Francisco Garcia

Juan Otero

Luciano Garcia

Isidro Otero

José Manuel Bustos

José Antonio Romero

Juan Montoya

Juan José Romero

Manuel Torres

Bian Torres

Santiago Lucero

José Sanchez y Torres

Toribio Mirabal

Lorenzo Torres

Antonio José Luera

Luis Flores

Cipriano Torres

Manuel Sanchez y Chavez

Nicolas Torres

Surveyor General's Office
Santa Fe, New Mexico

May 18, 1959

The foregoing is a correct translation of the original file in this office.

(Signed) David Whitney
Translator

*This document I copied from the files of the Manzano Land Grant Commission.

APPENDIX II

RULES AND REGULATIONS OF THE MANZANO WATER COMMISSION*

"First: The Treasurer will be paid at the rate of 5% of the monies with which he may be entrusted as Treasurer.

"Second: The Secretary will be paid at the rate of $1.50 for each time he furnishes the water boss with a list of people assigned for work, also for keeping the records of office.

"Third: The President will be paid at the rate of 10 cents for each time that he may call a meeting, on condition that such a meeting is held.

"Fourth: None of these officers will be entitled to these reimbursements if they have not bonded according to law.

"Fifth: These reimbursements will be made from the treasurer's fund, provided there are funds available, at the time the officers are replaced by the newly elected. If there are no funds, they will be given credit on their share of the work.

"Sixth: The commissioners in force will be in charge of the records, documents, and monies, if any, until their successors have been duly qualified for the office.

"Seventh: The Commission will have the right to assess the amount of work or its equivalent to each owner of land under irrigation or water-user, whichever it may be.

"<u>Eighth</u>: The Water Commission will furnish the water boss with the necessary assessment lists.

"<u>Duties of the Water Boss</u>

"It will be the duty of the water boss in conjunction with the Commission and the people to watch and care for all the reservoir, main ditches, laterals, and head and lateral gates.

"It will be his duty to notify the people for work at least one day in advance, if it is possible, according to the lists furnished him by the Commission. He will not permit the use of water to any person who may refuse or may fail to put in his share of labor or pay his assessed equivalent, as per order of the Commission.

"All the monies received by him in lieu of work, or in water rights, or fines, in other words, all monies received in relation to water use, shall be delivered to the Secretary of the Commission, who shall receipt the same, enter and deliver to the Treasurer, who shall acknowledge receipt of same.

"In case any person should want to buy surplus water or the right to use the water, the water boss must consult the Commission before making the sale.

"The water boss will receive as payment for his services $1.00 per person for irrigation. (This was amended later to $1.50 for alfalfa fields and 50 cents for gardens. This last figure was later changed to 75 cents). He is to be paid 25 cents at the beginning of the season and the balance before the last of October with either produce or money. (The last date was later amended to read 25 cents at the beginning and the balance before the 15th of July).

"First: The first duty of the Commission and water boss is to protect the springs of water and then do whatever work is recommended by the commission.

"Second: a 'water right' will be known as 'one day of water' or a 'water right' is whereby assessed by the commission at a rate of 6 days of work and each day shall be valued at $1.50 which shall be in lieu of work.

The Irrigation Ditches of Manzano

"1. Acequia del Medio, or middle ditch. This originates at the base of the tank and drains the Arroyo del Bosque.

"2. Acequia del Rancho del Lopez, or the ditch of Lopez's ranch. This ditch takes its water from the middle ditch after this middle ditch passes the Arroyo de Los Pinos Reales. This ditch drains into the Arroyo Chato after passing through the upper part and south of Los Ojitos.

"3. Acequia del Alto, or upper ditch. This ditch takes its water from the middle ditch, also from the tank, and drains at the end of the cultivated land, southwest of the Cerrito del Llano.

"4. Acequia del Molino, or ditch of the water mill. The water for this ditch originates on the north side of the tank directly from the spring, and passes on the outside of the town until it reaches the Tanque de la Joya, the old reservoir."

*This description of the duties of the Manzano Water Commission was copied from the Docket of Water Facilities Administration, Soil Conservation Service, Albuquerque.

APPENDIX III

THE MANZANO FIESTA, 1938

The description of the fiesta that follows was one that I witnessed in 1938 (Figure XXI). In the morning visitors from nearby settlements and villages began to filter in by wagon, in cars of the Model T vintage and on horseback. The main activity was centered in and around the construction of several frame and canvas stands from which were dispensed hot dogs, lemonade and typical carnival types of items like plaster of paris dolls. These stands were overshadowed by a large tent with a poster advertising a group of Spanish-American clowns and actors from Albuquerque. Beside this tent was a smaller one in which the usual games of chance were installed. The only Anglo-American participating in the commercial endeavors was a very large man from California in a decrepit car buying old gold and repairing watches. As can be expected the two local stores and the cantina did a good business during the preparation for the fiesta.

Several men, the padrinos, of the church placed small piles of cut juniper wood known as luminarios, along the churchyard wall to be burned that night. The fiesta officially began at twelve o'clock noon with the firing of a rifle. Miguel Lovato, an old Spanish-American troubadour, with his ancient violin and another musician with a guitar began playing in front of the church door. After playing several century-old melodies for about fifteen minutes they retired to the saloon.

In the afternoon the crowds began to pour in, nearly all them being Spanish-Americans of the region. Little formal activity occurred in the afternoon, a period devoted mainly to drinking in the cantina, buying trinkets from the stand and playing penny-ante behind walls and automobiles. By evening a large number of the people were becoming intoxicated, including the musicians who had to play later in the church.

At seven o'clock in the evening the church bells began to ring, calling the devout to vespers. Slowly the people filed into the church. Inside the building were profuse decorations such as paper flowers, a small nativity scene in front of the altar, Christmas tree glass balls and long strings of other kinds of Christmas ornaments. The male participants were dressed in many kinds of clothing, the best that they could afford, overalls contrasting with new suits. All the older women wore the typical formal dress that included a black shawl, high black shoes and black dresses.

The services began with the musicians, who were intoxicated, being helped up the steps of the choir loft. The choir was composed mainly with old women who sang in the high, nasal style typical of Spanish-American church choirs. Their voices contrasted unfavorably with the old troubadour's excellent music. The atmosphere was charged with the religious fervor of the audience, slightly tempered with the loud crying of several babies.

For nearly an hour the services continued with a recurring series of violin and guitar selections and singing by the choir. At the conclusion the congregation filed out of the church, which had been filled to capacity and people were standing at the door and in the aisles. The luminarios in the churchyard and the plaza were then lighted and a brilliant scene resulted with the smell of the burning juniper and the crowds standing around the fires to keep warm even though it was early fall. After a while bands from the two dance halls began to play loudly to attract the people, each playing different melodies. The music of each was good but the mixture was decidedly discordant.

The crowd split into two parties, the largest group going to the north dance hall. Nearly everyone danced, including small children who could barely walk and old men and women. Most of the people were good dancers, having a smooth step. Lacking always the opportunity for mixed dancing the boys danced with each other and so did the girls. "Dates" were scarce as it is the custom for Spanish-Americans of the region to attend dances accompanied by members of the same sex. The couples who came to the dance were mainly married. Few Anglo-Americans were present. For each dance the couples paid a dime.

The orchestra in the north dance hall sat on a high wood platform. The musicians had a cornet, saxophone, drum, accordion and guitar which were well played. This dance hall is long, low and rectangular with a rough board floor and a viga [wood cross beams] ceiling. Few windows grace the building whose only furnishing besides the orchestra platform consists of a long encircling bench. There are two side entrances besides the main entrance. In the small room on the south side of the structure was a large still, a relic of Prohibition days. The dance lasted far into the night during which time the usual drunken brawl occurred. Two drunks set off a commotion and in a short time half of the dancers were in an uproar, with men fighting with sticks and fists. One man, severely beaten on the head, had to be carried out.

On the next morning about nine o'clock mass was celebrated. Two visiting _padres_ aided in the services with one of them giving a sermon in Spanish from the side altar. After mass the outside procession began. In the lead were the musicians with three cornets and a drum playing marches and popular music. Following them was an old man carrying a cross on a long staff and behind him the participants walked in two long lines. Between these columns, near the front, walked the violin and guitar players. Further back four small girls carried on a litter the flower-decorated statue of the patron saint, Nuestra Señora de Dolores. Behind them in between the columns walked one of the two priests accompanied by two altar boys; then came the other visiting priests. At the very end was the local priest, Padre Guatier. The procession wound around the west end of Manzano, coming back to the church on the south side of the plaza. Then the people went back into the church and chanted a Latin prayer. After this the crowd dispersed. Dancing began anew and continued through the day and late into the night. A brief intermission occurred in the evening while the people retired to eat. With the end of the dances the fiesta terminated. Many little children occupied themselves during the fiesta by playing penny-ante in the alleys.

APPENDIX IV

INDITA DE MANUELITO

    This song was written by a poet of Torreón named Señor Chavez in the nineteenth century. It is still sung by old men in Manzano. Manuelito was an Apache chief killed by American soldiers and was considered to be a friend of the people of Manzano.

Indita de Manuelito Con qué sentimientos estas. Que en El Ojo de Gallina Que mataron debajo de paz.	Ballad of Manuelito With what sentiments you are. Who at the Ojo de Gallina Was killed during a truce.
No te mataron peleando Ni tampoco a bien a bien. Que mataron a traición, Charley el Capitan Gray.	They didn't kill you fighting Nor by honorable means Who was killed treacherously, By Charley, the Captain Gray.
Yo soy el Indio Manuel Que el mundo cause ruin. Yo me vivo depurado En El Ojo de Gallina. Por beber un trago De whiskey de una cantina.	I am the Indio Manuel Who causes ruin to the world. I live a purified life At the Spring of Gallina. I drink a large swallow Of whiskey from a canteen.
Yo soy el Indio Manuel El hermano de Mariano Que con la flecha en el mano Empalmó de dos o tres Sea Indio, sea Cristiano, Americano, o Frances.	I am the Indian Manuel The brother of Mariano Who with the arrow in my hand Impales two or three Whether Indian, Christian, American, or French.
Charley se reclamo sus bueyes, Balido de ocasión Y le respondio el Bacon, Oh, Charley no me da sus bueyes, ¿No es esa tu religión? No lo permiten tus leyes.	Charley recovered his oxen, Taking advantage of the opportunity And Bacon answered him, "Oh, Charley don't give me your oxen, Isn't that your religion? Your laws don't permit it."
Adiós, todos mis amigos, Ya se muere Manuelito. Ya ni pelearon conmigo La gente de Manzanito.	Goodbye, all my friends, Manuelito is now dying, You didn't fight with me You people of Manzano.

Para cantar esta indita
Del Apache Manuelito
Para cantar la bonito
Como lo canto el le quito
Al primero toque de diana
Un dia en el Rio Bonito.

Gobernador de Santa Fe,
Tú mi muerte te declaras
Y mantienes de cafe
Porque nunca me alzara.
Varios bueyes me robó,
Para que tu los pagaras.

In order to sing this ballad
Of the Apache Manuelito
In order to sing the beautiful
As he sang it he [died?]
At the time of reveille
One day on the Rio Bonito.

Governor of Santa Fe,
My death you declared.
You are sustained by coffee
So that I would never run away
You robbed me of several oxen
You will have to pay for them.

INDITA DE AMADO CHAVEZ*

En mil novecientos y dos	In the year 1902
Algo tenemos que hablar	We have something to say
Me despido de este mundo	I take leave of this world
De mi patria y de mi hogar.	From my fatherland and my home.
Dia veinte y uno de agosto	The 21th day of August
Quiso la alta prudencia	High prudence willed that
Que me fuera de esta vida	I should leave this life
A la otra arendir mis cuentas.	To the other to settle my accounts.
Me despido de mis padres	I take leave of my parents
Con la major resistencia.	With greatest resistance.
Con a los dos de la tarde	At about two o'clock in the afternoon
Me despido sin demora.	I take my leave without delay.
Y hice una resolución	And I made a resolution
De esta vida transitoria	In this transitory life
Para dar la cuenta a Dios	To settle my accounts with God
Y deseoso de vivir a su gloria.	And desirous of living in glory.
Don Jesús María Chavez	Don Jesús Maria Chavez
Y Nestorito Romero	And Nestorito Romero
Sintiendo en sus corazones	Feeling in their hearts
Y dicen haciendo en duelo	And expressing their sorrow.
Ya se fue el quien nos mostraba	He who used to show all of us
Cariño al mundo entero.	Affection in the entire world.

The song continues with various tributes to his friends and to the
places where they live such as at Manzano, Punta de Agua, Los Chaves,
Tomé and Los Gabaldones.

*Amado Chavez was a well-known New Mexico politician descended from
one of the families who accompanied De Vargas reconquest of New Mexico
in 1698. He was born in 1851. He held both federal and state offices
between 1876 and 1912 (Lange and Riley 1970:411).

EL BORRACHO

Vente borracho conmigo.
Yo te llevare a tu casa
Yo estimo mas mi botella
Que el ir a ver mi dama.

¿Que te paso borrachito?
Por andar en la cocina
Te pelo la cocinera
Creyendo que eres gallina.
¿Que te paso borrachito?

Por andar en la cantina
Pegando gritos e guapo
Y tu mujer sin harina.

Come drunkard with me.
I will take you home
I esteem more my bottle
Than going to see my girl.

What has happened little drunkard?
Because you were in the kitchen
That the cook plucked you
Thinking that you are a chicken.
What is happening to you little
 drunkard?
Because you were in the bar
Yelling like a tough guy
And your women without flour.

INDITA DE MANUEL B. OTERO

Amigos de Tajique, de Torreón
Y Manzano, tambien de Punta de Agua
Concurran a mi amor.

Ano de mil ochocientos ochenta y
    dos
Al contado se vió Manuelito Otero
En sus sangres revolcado
En ese rancho de Estancia,
Que rancho tan desgraciado.

Dice Manuelito Otero
Con sus palabras de honor.
Whitney enseñame el derecho
Para estar en mi possession

Por si tienes derecho
No quiero tener question.

Whitney le respondió
De colera perseguido.
Derecho no tengo yo
Ni nunca lo he concecido.
O te sales de este rancho
A mis armas rendidos.

Fernandez se entremetió
De un tiro su consuelo
Y en un momento quedó bajo
De las patas de Otero.
Su crimen lo castigó
Todos deben conocelo.

Whitney se quería apropriar.
De su ley fisica empuño
Pero Otero le salió
Encontra de su fortuna
Porque Otero le salió
Cambiando dos por una.

Dos hermanos que
Y conmigo somos tres
Yo que les prometí

Friends of Tajique, of Torreon,
And Manzano, also of Punta de Agua
Concur with my love.

In the year eighteen hundred and
    eighty two
Immediately Manuelito Otero is seen
Wallowing in his blood
In that ranch of Estancia.
What a wretched ranch.

Says Manuelito Otero
With his words of honor.
Whitney show me the law
That gives you the right
    to be on my property
For if you have the right
I will not argue with you.

Whitney responded to him
Overcome with anger.
Right I do not have
Nor have I ever known it.
You get off this ranch
Having surrendered to my arms.

Fernandez butted in
With a shot as his advice
And in a moment fell under
The feet of Otero.
He was punished for his crime
Everyone must know.

Whitney wished to take possession.
He had recourse to physical force
But Otero came out [to fight him?]
Against his fortune
Because Otero left him
Exchanging two for one.

Two brothers who
And with me three
I who they promised

Defender con rapidez.	To defend quickly.
Pienso que les cumpli.	I think I did my duty.
Mi muerte será un confusion.	My death will be a confusion.

Don Carlos por su desgracia	Don Carlos to his misfortune
Estar sin armas se hallo.	Found himself without arms.
Tomo pluma en la mano	He took a pen in hand
Y las muertes escribio.	And about the deaths wrote.

Adios, hermanos mayores	Goodbye, my best friends
Don Jesus y Don Tranquilo	Don Jesus and Don Tranquilo
Ahi les encargo mis flores	I assign to you my flowers
De ese bien concebido.	Of my well conceived favor.

En la plaza de Los Lunas	In the plaza of Los Lunas
Deje todo mi hermosuras.	I left all my beautiful things.
Deje mi cruz y mi anhelo.	I leave my cross and my desire.
¿Que es la mas grande dulzura?	Which is the greatest sweetness?

Adios, Adios Eloisa querida.	Goodbye, goodbye dear Eloisa
Se acaba todo tu haver	All your property has been used up
Que tu esposo de partida.	That your husband has left.
No lo olvides a ver	Don't forget to see
Con la mas grande fatiga	With the greatest worrysomeness
Lo vinistes a saber.	That you came to see.

De Los Lunas y Tomé	Of Los Lunas and Tome´
De Torreón y de Manzano	Of Torreón and Manzano
Tambien de la Punta de Agua	And also Punta de Agua
Vinieron muy amado.	They came very lovely.

Dice Manuelito Otero	Manuelito Otero says
A que desgraciada sombra	Oh what an unfortunate shadow
Por defenderme derecho.	For defending my rights.
Mi familia quedo sola	My family remained alone
Pero sin consuelo	But without joy
Porque es vida sin honor.	Because it is a life without honor.

Adios de los Tome	Goodbye they of Tome
En que yo me recriaba.	In which I used to enjoy myself.
Si algo les iba a su pueblito	If something happened to your town
me remediaba.	I will take care of it.

Adios, Eloisa lucida	Goodby, magnificent Eloisa
Querida de mi corazon.	Beloved of my heart.
Hay ten cargo de mis hijitos.	Take care of my children.
Dar les buena educacion.	Give them a good education.

Adios, Eloisa lucida	Goodbye magnificent Eliosa
Don Tranquilo y Salamon,	Don Tranquilo and Solomon.
Tus seras la protegida	You will be the protegee
Haciendo la administracion.	Doing the administration.

Ante Dios pongo mi queja	Before God I place my complaint
Supremo tribunal	Supreme tribunal
Si ha de juzgarme mi querida.	If he is to judge me, my dear.

En una cortemarcial.   In a courtmartial.
Porque mi derecho es bueno   Because my rights are good
Y mi tratado legal.   And my case legal.

Adios, Madre y Sabelita   Goodby, mother and Sabelita.
Adios, porque ya me voy.   Goodby because I am going.
Pero muy agradecido de   Because I am grateful
Buen lugar que me dio.   For the good place she gave me.

Esta indita esta compuesta   This ballad is composed
Por Casamiro Lujan.   By Casamiro Lujan.
A salud de los dolientes [?]   Health to the suffering people
Y del pueblo en general   And to people in general
Que los jovenes valientes   Because the valiant young
Dejen algo que pensar.   Leave you something to think about.

Chorus

Indita de Manuel B.   Ballad of Manuel B.
Resenti en la constancia   Resentful in the constancy
Por defender tu derecho   In defending your right
Sufristes muertes sin causa.   You suffered deaths without cause.

Note: The fight described above occurred at Estancia Springs. Whitney was not mortally wounded. Killed were Manuel B. Otero, the son of Manuel A. Otero, who claimed he had bought the Estancia Land Grant from Gov. Baca. Also killed was Alexander Fernandez, a brother-in-law of James B. Whitney (Lange and Riley, 1970:4).

RIDDLES AND PROVERBS

Below is a riddle written by Casamiro Lujan of Torreon:

En el día en que nací	On the day that I was born
En la hora me bautisaron	At that the hour I was baptized
En el día pedí mujer	In the same day I asked for a wife
En el mismo me casaron.	In the same day they married me.
Mi madre es una criatura	My mother is a creature
Que no tiene entendimiento	Who has no understanding
Ni luz ni conocimiento.	Neither light or knowledge.
No puede hablar	She could not speak
Porque es muda.	Because she is mute.
Mi padre imagen pura	My father a pure image
Y encomprensible así.	And thus incomprehensible
Que habiéndome tenido a mi	That having taken me
Solo me llamo' al mundo.	Alone into the world.
Esto es cierto y verdadero	This is certain and true
Come dice la escritura	As the scripture says
Que para formarme	In order to form me
Abrieron mi sepultura	They opened my grave
Y mi vida es tal altura	And my life is so lofty
Que los hombres adoraron.	That the men adore me.
En el mundo cuando viví	In the world when I lived
Con quatro letras me hablaron.	With four letters they addressed me.

Answer Adam [Adam]

When the matachines dancers performed at Manzano, although there is no evidence they were a local group, riddles were told. Below are two examples,

A male dancer said, "Mariano está en el llano, tiene cruzes y no es Cristiano." [Mariano is of the plains, he has crosses but is not a Christian.] Answer: El entraña [a type of cactus?].

A female dancer said, "Ella tiene cuatro patas y sola mano." [She has four feet and one hand.] Answer: el metate [a grinding stone].

Below are other riddles told at Manzano,

Largo, pelado y en la punta doblado. [Long, bare and doubled at the point]. Answer: la reata [rope].

Una vaca pinta paso por el mar bramidos sin ser animal. [A colored cow goes through the sea bellowing without being an animal]. Answer: las nubes [clouds].

Below are other proverbs from Manzano,

No todas las veces se besa al santo. [Not all the time can you kiss the saint]. This means that not all the time is man's luck with him, a saying derived from the local Catholic custom of kissing the saint's feet on Corpus Cristi day.

El que boca tiene a Roma va. [He who can talk will get to Rome].

Ya despues de conejo fuido piedras al matoral. [After the rabbit flees you can only throw rocks into the bushes].

El gato que tiene guantes no agarra ratones. [The cat that wears gloves doesn't catch the mice].

Calma tambien sus tormentos y halla dicha verdadera cuando se muestra contento con lo que tiene y espera. [Calm your torments and find truth when you are content with what you have and have hope].

FOLKTALES AND SUPERSTITIONS

The owl

At one time there lived a bird with no feathers called hu-hu. An owl took pity on the poor bird and called a meeting of all the birds. At this reunion the owl persuaded each bird to give a feather to the hu-hu. After receiving the feathers the hu-hu became a very beautiful and vain creature. Scorning the company of the other birds the hu-hu flew away. All these birds became infuriated with the owl, attacked him and demanded that he retrieve all the feathers of the hu-hu. This story explains why the owl will not come out in the daytime for he is afraid of the other birds. It also explains why other birds attack the owl and why he goes around calling "hu-hu" as he tries to get the feathers back.

El escorpión

The common collared lizards, Crotaphytus colaris, who run sometimes on their hind legs, are called los escorpiones at Manzano. Although this lizard is actually harmless it is believed that its bite can be deadly poisonous. Local tales abound of lizards jumping on the necks of sheep and urinating on them, an action believed to cause the deaths of the animals. One villager told me that one time in the Manzano Mountains one of these lizards chased him for over a half mile. When he finally got so

tired he had to stop and fortunately the lizard also stopped and then
went away.

Other superstitions

One time some men from Punta de Agua and Chato were in the
mountains rounding up their cattle. Suddenly they saw a very hairy
fearful-looking man. But then a nice-looking man went up to the hairy
man and began to talk. The cattlemen fled in fright.

The campmocha [praying mantis] is belived to be deadly poisonous to
livestock if it gets into their food and is eaten.

When a shooting star is seen the Manzaneños say "Jesús te guia."
[Jesus is guiding you].

PLACE OF BIRTH OF SPANISH-AMERICANS OF THE MANZANO VOTING PRECINCT OVER

TWENTY-ONE YEARS OF AGE, 1939*

Torrance County	
Name of town	Number of voters
Abó...3	
Estancia..2	
La Cienega......................................2	
Manzano.......................................256	
Mountainair.....................................2	
Palma...1	
Pinos Altos.....................................1	
Punta de Agua...................................6	
Tajique...3	
Torreón...3	
Willard...6	
Progreso..4	
Subtotal......291	
Other counties in New Mexico	
Albuquerque.....................................1	
Anton Chico.....................................2	
Belen...3	
Casa Colorado...................................1	
Carrizozo.......................................2	
Chilili...1	
Galisteo..1	
La Joya...3	
Las Vegas.......................................1	
Lincoln...6	
Montezuma.......................................2	
Nutrias...1	
Pena Blanca.....................................1	
Picacho...1	
Pueblo Blanco...................................1	
Rabenton..2	
Ruidosa...3	
Sabinal...1	
Santa Fe..1	
San Fernando....................................1	
San Juan..2	
San Marcial.....................................1	
San Pablo.......................................1	

```
            San Antonio....................................1
            San Rafael.....................................1
            Socorro........................................1
            Taos...........................................1
            Tomé.......................................:...9
            Tularosa.......................................2
            Wagon Mound....................................1
            Vadenos........................................1
            Valencia.......................................1
            Valverde.......................................1
```

Total voters born in other counties........................61
Total voters born outside of Manzano......................96
Percent of Manzano voters born outside of village........36.66
Total number of Spanish-American voters..................352
*Information taken from list in County Clerk's Office in Estancia

NUMBER OF PEOPLE PER ROOM AT MANZANO

Number of rooms	Number of houses	Total rooms
1	4	4
2	25	50
3	25	75
4	15	60
5	2	10
Total	71	199

Number of members in each household											Total people
1	2	3	4	5	6	7	8	9	10	11	
0	1	2	1	0	0	0	0	0	0	0	12
0	3	7	4	4	3	2	1	1	0	0	111
2	2	8	2	4	0	3	2	0	0	2	117
0	2	1	3	2	0	2	3	1	1	0	32
0	0	0	1	0	0	1	0	0	0	0	11

Total people.......333

Average number of people per room.....................1.670

WORDS OF MEXICAN-INDIAN AND LOCAL ORIGIN USED AT MANZANO

Aquajalote: water dog; mixed Spanish and Aztec derivation.

Arco: the rainbow, also a bow; Spanish origin.

Alvarones: alternate form of chicharones [cracklings]; Spanish origin?

Atole: a thick gruel-like beverage made of corn and water and slightly
    sweetened; from American Indian atolli (Bently 1932)).

Beyota: wood knot; unknown derivation.

Burro: in addition to the animal it is a sawhorse; Spanish origin.

Cacique: a village chief; derived from West Indies.

Caciquismo: the control of community votes by a dominant individual.

Camino del cielo: the Milky Way; Spanish origin.

Capulin: chokecherries, Aztez derivation.

Carreta: cart; also the Great Dipper; Spanish origin.

Chahuiste: corn blight; Mexican-Indian origin.

Chanentes: blackbirds; possible Spanish origin.

Chapulin: locusts or grasshoppers derived from Aztec.

Chupalote: buzzard; derived from Aztec zopilotl.

Comal: a rectangular clay box used for cooking, also a flat clay or
    stone griddle; Aztec origin.

Cintela: a thin sheep; Spanish origin.

Culebra chirronera: local snake with black back and red and white
    stomach; unknown origin.

Culebra mamona: milk snake; unknown origin.

Durmilon: the bird known as nighthawk; probably Spanish origin.

Estrella de ocasion: the Evening Star; Spanish origin.

Esquite: roasted whole corn mixed with salt; Indian origin.

Galletos: bisquits made from medium ground wheat mixed with beef; Spanish origin?

Haspe or yeso: burnt gypsum used as a whitewash for houses; possibly Spanish origin.

Jacal: house with vertical post walls; Mexican-Indian origin.

Lovera: bear trap; derivation unknown.

Lucero: Mars; Spanish origin.

Mano: a stone held in the hand to grind corn on a slab [metate]. Word Spanish in origin.

Mantas: clothing made of flour sacks; Spanish origin.

Malacate: spindle whorl; Aztec origin.

Marana: a hog; possibly Spanish origin.

Matachine: a mixed Spanish-American-Mexican Indian dance celebrating the conquest of the Aztecs by Cortez. Performed by Indians and Spanish-Americans of New Mexico.

Metraca: bull roarer used by the Penitentes. In Mexico it is a wheel with a clapper and used in a church belfry. It is also a crank-shaped tool made of wood for winding horsehair to make rope and cord. It is held taut. Origin of word unknown.

Mecate: rope; possibly of Mexican-Indian origin.

Metate: a stone used for grinding corn by hand; Aztec origin.

Milpa: a small plot of land used for agriculture; Mexican-Indian origin.

Pinole: a gruel-like beverage made from parched corn and mixed with sweetening; from American Indian pinolli (Bently 1932:167).

Tapeiste: a wood platform for drying food; Mexican-Indian origin.

Tepanco: a wood and adobe bench in a kitchen; probably Aztec origin.

Tequas: moccasins; possibly Mexican-Indian origin.

Tepalcate: pot sherd; Aztec origin.

Tepacate: tadpole; Aztec origin.

Tortilla: a flat cake made of corn; Word Spanish.

Tortillas de nixtamal: blue corn tortillas; Aztec origin.

<u>Trobo</u>: a series of verses sung by troubadours from memory; Spanish.

<u>Tremetina</u>: pine pitch, turpentine; Spanish.

<u>Sacate</u>: hay; Aztec origin.

<u>Sacahuiste</u>: bear grass; Aztec origin.

<u>Vivuela</u>: a musical string bow; probably Spanish origin.

LUCAS ZAMORA

One of the oldest men at Manzano was Lucas Zamora who was born on
October 10, 1856, in Casa Colorado, while his wife, Porfiria was born
May, 1866. His parents were José Jesús Zamora and Isabelita Maldonado.
His grandfather, a Spanish nobleman, founded the village of Casa
Colorada in the Rio Grande Valley on a land grant from the King of
Spain. Lucas claims to be a relative of the former president of Spain,
Alcario Zamora. The photographs of his parents reveal them to be people
of distinction. His grandmother was a beautiful women with blond hair,
large blue eyes and had the poise of a refined gentlewoman. Her clothing
appeared to be expensive; in addition to a gems-studded tiara in her
hair she also wore several pieces of other ornate jewelry. Lucas states
that these jewels were stolen by Indians.

Lucas states the he remembers his grandfather vividly, that he was
a gentleman and a scholar and that he spoke perfect Spanish and taught
Lucas all that he knew since Lucas had no formal education. Lucas's
speech reveals the influence of Classic Spanish in his use of phrases,
unusual at Manzano such as "viendo tiempo" [as time came] and "yendo
tiempo" [as time passed]. Lucas's behavior can best be described as that
of a courtly gentleman. The grandfather was very wealthy for his day,
having large herds of cattle. Many times the Navajo Indians drove some
of the cattle away. It was not unusual for some of the livestock to
return with arrows in their backs.

When Lucas was several months old his father died and the Zamora family moved to Manzano where his mother married again. When Lucas was eleven years old his grandparents died and he felt that no one cared for him anymore. His step-father treated him and his mother so badly that he left home. He married Porfiria Candelaria at Manzano in 1861. She was born and raised there and attended several grades of school. She is able to read, write and speak Spanish very well. The Zamoras never had any children.

Lucas Zamora by Manzano standards is about medium in income and property. He owns 30 acres, with 15 in cultivation, 2 horses, 3 milk cows, 8 range cows and 25 chickens.

At the time when Lucas was a small boy Manzano did not have more than 100 inhabitants. Lucas saw his first fight betweeen Indians and the people of Manzano when he was 7 or 8 years old. The fight, which occurred at night, was provoked by Indians trying to steal horses. In Manzano there was a big drum that was beaten when an attack by Indians was imminent. Another way of warning was given by a man who slept on a roof and who yelled when he saw Indians approaching. The Manzaneños often scalped dead Indians and the Indians did likewise. Lucas witnessed scalps brought to Manzano and displayed on a pole. In celebration a dance was held. Sometimes the scalps, attached to a pole, were taken to Torreón and Tajique.

At the time when his grandparents died and he was eleven years old he was herding and driving cattle from Fort Bliss, Texas to Roswell, Trinidad and Denver. He worked for a Texan named Sloan and earned about $45.00 a month and had the use of two horses. On the cattle drives they traveled on horses accompanied by oxcarts. When they returned from Denver they brought back the provisions for Sloan's cattle ranch. A

cook always was present in the cattle drives. At that time his friends
were Anglo-American cowboys from Texas and New Mexico. On these trips he
cried a lot for his mother. He next got a job with John Buhlen of Belen
and hauled sacks of wool in an ox cart to Fort Sheldon, Colorado, where
he sold the cargo to Miguel Otero and a man named Brown. On the return
to Belen he traveled via Trinidad, Wagon Mound, Las Vegas, the Estancia
Valley and Abó Canyon, a trip that took about five months.

He bought a wagon and a yoke of oxen when he was fourteen years old
and joined a caravan that hauled supplies from Kansas to all parts of
the west. On some of the trips he hauled coffee from Tuscon and traded
it for supplies at Dodge City, then known as Fort Dodge. It took four to
five months to make the round trip. At that time Dodge City was the
largest trading post west of the Mississippi. When Lucas was there teams
of horses and wagons formed lines as long as a mile around each
warehouse. At that time there were no railroads in that part of the
country. The freighters hauled supplies at the rate of four to five
cents a pound according to distance. In the stores the cheapest grade of
coffee sold for 50 cents a pound.

In the drives he encountered many Comanche Indians and was
friendly with one of their chiefs. The Comanches were distinguished from
other Plains Indians by the fine pinto ponies they rode. They were armed
with lances that had points made of flint and metal. Their chief wore a
white buffalo skin. Somewhat later the Plains Indians became very
warlike and many Spanish-Americans became afraid to make the trip. After
he bought five wagons and was in charge of two more it took him several
days to locate enough employees. He finally located two men in Socorro,
three in Manzano and an old friend that had traveled with him before.
They carried fifty pound sacks of ammunition, twenty-five thousand

rounds each, several 35-45 rifles, forty-four other rifles and several six shooters. They never saw any Indians until their return from Dodge City. On the last lap of their journey from Socorro to Hot Springs they came upon three large burning wagons belonging to other freighters which the Indians had robbed and slain the people. Seeing that no one was alive they hurried on to the little village of Las Animas. The settlement had been ransacked and all the windows and doors of the houses were open. There was no sign of life and blood was splattered all over the rooms. Lucas and his companions hurried on to Las Cruces. On their return to Socorro they heard loud noises and drawing near they saw U.S. Army soldiers throwing their caps in the air and yelling at the tops of their voices. They had captured and killed many of the Apaches responsible for the raid.

In 1872 when he was 17 years old he went on his first buffalo hunt with Pablo Fricas, nephew of Padre Sembrano, the Catholic priest at Manzano. They traveled in ox carts with covered tops. Pablo was older than Lucas and promised to teach him how to hunt buffalo. In the party were many ciboleros [buffalo hunters]. They left Manzano and ran into buffalo near Portales. At an earlier time the buffalo had roamed in the Estancia Valley but had all been killed off. The hunters used long lances that had a wood handle and a steel point. They would charge the buffalo on horses. When ready to kill them they would find a point on the animal by counting down three ribs from the shoulder and stab them there.

At that time the area of Portales was occupied by Comanches. Groups of five or six of these Indians would ride up to Lucas's party and ask for flour, coffee and sugar. They would give the Indians their requests because they wanted to preserve friendly relations with this tribe.

When the first suitable buffalo herd was spotted Lucas chased one animal with his horse and stabbed it in the shoulder. Unfortunately he neglected to pull his lance out. He rode back to Pablo rejoicing for he thought that he had killed his first bison. Pablo asked him after he got over his excitement where the buffalo was. When Lucas looked around the animal was nowhere to be seen. Pablo then erupted in a stream of curses. To vindicate himself Lucas set out on a search for the buffalo and found him in deep grass in a draw bleeding from the lance which was still in the shoulder. The animal was on his front knees, the position the bison take when they are dying. As he neared the animal it suddenly rose with bloodshot eyes and charged him. Lucas, fortunately, had another lance with him and stabbed the animal in the neck in front of the shoulder, killing it just in time. For this act he was taken back with good graces into the hunting party. This was the first bison killed and eaten on the trip.

After a large number of bison were killed they were laid out on the ground and skinned by cutting down the belly and pulling off from the neck downwards. The hides were not saved and the meat was loaded into the wagons which held from 30 to 35 animals. On hunting trips there usually were from twelve to fourteen wagons.

While hunting a group of about 14 Indians tried to steal their horses but they were caught before they had success. These Indians lived in dome-shaped shelters made of bent poles and buffalo hide covers.

When he was 18 years old his father took him on another hunting trip. They traveled into the area of Tucumcari and to the region of Palo Amarillo. This was a very successful trip and each wagon was loaded with 45 bison. Lucas killed 78 of these animals. In these areas they also saw many antelope and wild horses. This was the last hunt from Manzano for reason that the wasteful slaughter of the bison was polluting the waterholes and streams and the animals were becoming very rare.

From 1873 to 1881 Lucas continued his work freighting goods to and from Dodge City. In September, 1880, he left Las Vegas for Silver City. As he was traveling through the Mimbres Valley he saw many Indian footprints. Arriving at Las Animas he saw that the village had been burned again and the people killed by Indians. Rumors were that the Indians escaped to Mexico. When he arrived, however, at Silver City he found everyone celebrating for the chiefs of the Apache raiders, Victorio and Mangas Coloradas, had been killed.

He married in 1882 and he and his wife opened in the following year a general store in Manzano which he kept for 17 years and the post office for 7 years. He claims that his store was the largest one in the Estancia Valley. Lucas bought his goods in Santa Fe from a wholesaler by the name of Stapp, from Ilfelds in Albuquerque and Becker in Belen. He was very prosperous since he owned besides his store a saloon and a large ranch. This ranch was located in Red Canyon and the foreman of the ranch was an Anglo-American who was paid $100.00 a month plus his supplies. On this ranch he had many horses, sheep and cattle. He moved to his present ranch where he has lived for the last thirty-two years, during which time he raised crops. He had at one time a ranch to the east of the present one but it was confiscated by the government because he did not have any documents proving that he owned the land.

Lucas never had any children. He adopted Amalia Perea when she was six years old. Amalia is feeble-minded and has epileptic strokes. Also adopted is Anita Martinez, the daughter of Manuel Martinez who used to help the Zamoras on their farm. Manuel was arrested for bootlegging and is now in the New Mexico penitentiary.

APPENDIX XIV

JULIAN CHAVEZ

Julian Chavez, whose buffalo hunting trip has been described in the text of this report is an 80 year old man with courtly manners and who speaks the excellent Spanish of his generation (Figure XI). His only education was from a priest at Manzano who taught him how to read and write. He is a small slender man who is quite energetic in spite of having arthritis, bronchitis and heart trouble. He married into the Torres family on June 29, 1883. Mrs. Chavez is 70 years old and like Julian was born in Manzano. They have seven children and live with a daughter in a three room house in the small hamlet of Chato. He receives some support from the Old Age Assistance program.

Julian's parents were born in Valencia County of the central Rio Grande Valley but moved to Manzano before he was born since they obtained a land grant. He had four brothers, the two younger ones being good looking boys. Two Indians from Isleta were selling fruit at the Manzano fiesta. Unfortunately they had the mal ojos and stared at his younger brothers. The next night after the fiesta they became very sick. The eyes of one of his brothers came out of their sockets and hung against his cheeks by the nerves. In a short time these brothers died. When Julian was born he was very ugly for he had hair all over his body. His mother finally found a remedy to remove the hair. Julian is much more superstitious than most Manzaneños.

208

As a teenager he went to Lincoln County to work on a farm for $50.00 a month. At that time the area was embroiled in the infamous Lincoln County War in which Billy the Kid lost his life. Julian was witness to the following events: after the general store in Lincoln was burned MacSween, a member of one of the feuding families, was killed by a band of Texans who were pillaging the county. These bandits used to encircle the county returning to Fort Stanton where they were fed and given beds in the house of Charles Fritz. This man was afraid not to give them shelter. One time at supper these Texans announced that they were going to kill all the Mexicans in the county. Fritz begged them not to kill his Mexican laborers since their help was needed on his farm. This they agreed not to do. After breakfast they set out on their murderous quest. They first went to the store of the two Sahagun brothers where they helped themselves to everything they wanted. At that time Julian and a man named Lopez were cutting hay along a road. Julian's uncle rode up and told them the great danger they were in, advising them to leave. Julian was only 19 at the time and still very foolish. He told his uncle that he wanted to stay and get his work done. He did, however, get out his rifle and laid it in a wagon about 40 feet away so it would not get too hot from the sun.

After failing in his mission his uncle rode away grumbling to himself. Soon the Texans rode up on horses made a circle around Julian and his friend. These Texans spoke to them in fluent Spanish since they had learned the language from their Mexican wives. At that time there were no Anglo-American women in the area. The bandits demanded that Julian and Lopez give them their arms. They kept repeating that they had no arms for they knew that the Texans intended to kill them whether they gave up their rifles or not. Julian finally raised one hand and begged to speak a few words to them. The Texans agreed and Julian stated they were working for Charles Fritz and if they did not believe them they could ask Fritz. Luckily the bandits believed him. At that time the Texans had their Sharps rifles jammed into Julian's and Lopez's chests. The bandits left and went down the road a short distance where they encountered an old Mexican man and his two sons. They shot the two sons, spared the old man and took the livestock which they had been guarding. Then two of the Texans returned to Julian and Lopez who believed that they were going to be killed. As they were approaching Julian took his rifle from the wagon telling Lopez he intended to fight. Lopez begged him not to do this. The Texans rode a couple of wide circles around them, firing three or four shots. Fortunately none of them hit Julian and Lopez. After this, for unknown reasons, the bandits left the road and went away into a little valley. Julian said that the Texans did not know he had a rifle for he had it concealed under his coat.

He moved to Barranca Colorada [Red Canyon] in 1900 and acquired a farm. In 1933 he became too old to farm and moved to Chato to live with his daughter. He no longer cultivates his land at Barranca Colorada. Julian claims that he killed one man at Barranca Colorada. Since then in remorse he has devoted his life to the Catholic Church. At Barranca Colorada he also placed a cross on top of a hill and every year at a secret date he returns to this cross to repent. This enables him to "keep the devil away".

ADDITIONAL MAJOR INFORMANTS

Cesaria Candelaria

Cesaria Candelaria was born in 1866 (age 72) and lived all her life in Manzano. Her father was a sheepherder. Her education consisted of two years of school but she can not read or write Spanish or speak English. She married Nestor Candelaria, born in La Joya in 1885, who ran a general store and tavern in Manzano until 1924. He died in 1934. The Candelarias had 10 boys and 3 girls. All of them are dead except one married son and daughter who live in Manzano. She adopted a grandson of her son but this person is now married and no longer lives in her house. Because she is sick and needed help she adopted a granddaughter. At present she is supported by the Old Age Assistance program.

David Candelaria

David Candelaria, a man 72 years old, was an excellent informant since he is unusually interested in the history of Manzano and its traditional customs. He is also well informed on local remedies for sickness and injuries. Because of these interests and other personality traits David is considered to be a strange person by other Manzaneños. He never went to school but can read and write Spanish. He can not, however, speak English.

David was born in Manzano, February 23, 1866. His wife was born in 1872 of a family of 12 children. Most of his life he worked as a farmer.

In 1871 he took a trip to Chihuahua, but other than that he spent his life in Manzano. As a young man he used to like to hunt on Chupadero Mesa for antelope, mountain lions, turkeys, deer and bears. He never went on a buffalo hunt.

The David Candelarias had 15 children but only 3 survived infancy. They live in a three room house with their daughter, Viviana (born February 27, 1908) and a son, Manuel (born February 12, 1909) in the Canyon de Pinos Altos. Manuel worked for the Mckinley lumber company until it closed. Another son, Juan, is married and was for a time in the Civilian Conservation Corps. The son he lives with was employed in McKinley's sawmill until it closed. David owns ten acres of land, some of which can be irrigated. In the years from 1935 to 1939 he had complete crop failure. He also owns two cows. The Candelarias are partially supported by the Old Age Assistance program.

David is very much concerned over his health and grows medicinal herbs. He wears clothing typical of his age which includes a cowboy hat, overalls, gray work shirt and black oxfords.

Aurelio Chavez

At the time I interviewed him he was very sick and unable to give much information. He was born in the Rio Grande Valley near La Joya. One time while he was herding sheep in the Ladron Mountains he was taken captive by the Navajos but escaped ten days later.

Dolores Chavez

Dolores Chavez, age 34 years, is one of the landless Manzaneños who has to obtain private and public employment. He was born in 1904 in Manzano and his wife was born in 1909 in the same village. His skills are that of a truck driver and jack hammer operator who worked for the Chino copper mines near Hurley for $3.20 a day. He was laid off in March, 1938, although promised employment if the mines open up again. He was then forced to apply for federal relief. The Chavezes live in a four room house which they obtain rent free from Dolores's father. They have one son age 12. Other than a few chickens they have no personal property. Dolores's health is good but his wife has heart trouble and poor eyesight.

Narciso Gomez

He was born in Manzano in 1861 (age 77). His father and mother came from Tomé. He never went to school. When he was 12 years old he tried to ride a calf and was thrown. His right arm was broken in two places and he had to have it amputated.

He was married to Mercedes, who was born in 1874 and who went to school for one year. Hijeno (1924) and Herman (born 1925) were sons of a daughter married to Jesus Lopez and were given to the Gomezes to raise. They live in three rooms of a five room house rent free and owned by a son-in-law Canuto.

Narciso farmed for 20 years and in 1932 began herding sheep for George Muillon of Laguna Blanca. He had to quit after a few years when he began losing sheep due to failing eyesight. At present he and his wife are supported by the Old Age Assistance program. They are both devout Catholics.

Guadalupe Griego

Guadalupe Griego because of his age of 79 years has led a more adventurous life than most Manzaneños. He was born in Sabinal in the central Rio Grande Valley, the birthplace also of his father, while his mother was born in Casa Colorado of the same area. Guadalupe was baptized in Belen and then brought to Manzano by his parents when he was one year old. He was the oldest child and had five brothers and six sisters. He and his present wife, Leandra, live in Manzano with two of his sisters while one brother lives in Peralta. One of his sisters is married to David Candelaria.

In 1873 he began his career hauling freight between Mexico and California, employment that lasted for 12 years. On these trips he drove both ox and mule teams. Once when one of the freight caravans was traveling in the Capitan Mountains the drivers were attacked by a band of Indians. Sixteen of Guadalupe's companions were killed but he managed to escape on foot. The wagons were burned and the mules driven away. He married his first wife, Catalina, in 1890, but she died the first year.

Since 1885 he has farmed, worked in mines and been a carpenter. His last employment was hauling lumber for the McKinley sawmill. Four years ago he sold his 66 acre farm and all his equipment to pay for his doctor's bill of $515.00 and another debt of $158.99. He is ill with urinary trouble.

The Griegos live in a two room jacal and now have only three chickens. Guadalupe's son now provides him fuel, His wife, Leandra, takes in laundry to support the family. He also receives Old Age Assistance. His daughter gave him her oldest child when it was a baby and the Griegos are raising him. Guadalupe and his wife go to church regularly but he says he really has no religion other than believing that people should do good.

Manuel Griego

Manuel Griego, age 42, has had a varied work experience. He was born in Manzano in 1896 and his wife, in 1899 in Manzano. They have two girls and one boy. He completed the 6th grade and reads, writes and speaks English and his wife completed the 4th grade.

From 1909-1917 he worked as a cowpuncher near Cedarville, then joined the army and after discharge became a trackman for the railroad and was stationed at Willard. When he lost this job he entered the Civilian Conservation Corps. He also tried farming in the 1930s but the bad droughts forced him in 1935 to apply for federal relief. He belongs to the American Legion and was for two years a member of the County Commission.

Manuel owns 140 acres of land near Chato with 50 acres being cultivated, 3 horses, 3 cows, 1 pig, 16 chickens, 1 lister and 1 go-devil.

Carlos Gutierrez

Carlos, age 60, was born in Montezuma, a small hamlet near Gran Quivira, in 1878 and his wife, two years younger than he, was born in Manzano in 1880. They live in a four room adobe house and have four children, one of whom is a daughter suffering from arthritis. He farmed 80 acres of land and owns two horses, one cow and seven chickens. The droughts of the 1930s resulted in crop failure and since 1935 he has worked for the Works Projects Administration.

Felipe Gutierrez

Felipe is a young man of 35 years who has been barely self supporting. He was born in Manzano and his wife, 32 years old, was born in Abó. His family is scattered with his mother at Abó, two sisters in Red Canyon, one sister at Barranca Colorada and another living in Mountainair. He went to the third grade and speaks a little English while his wife speaks, reads and writes English. The have a seven year old son. They live in a two room jacal.

During the years 1925-1928 he worked for the railroad. Now he farms on the 120 acres he owns and on 20 acres of land rented from a man in Estancia. His crops failed in 1938. He said his land is worth $4.00 an acre. He also owns 2 small horses worth $40.00, 15 goats worth $3.00 a piece, 15 chickens, 1 pig, 1 wagon, 1 lister, 1 cultivator and 1 go-devil.

Ignacio Herrera

Ignacio Herrera, age 64 years, was born in Manzano and went to school there for two years while his wife was born in Lincoln where she went to school for two years. He has two brothers and one sister who live in Manzano. The Herreras had six children of whom one died. Three boys and a girl live in Manzano and another girl lives in Torreón.

Ignacio and his wife and youngest daughter live in a three room log house. He owns 57 acres, all of which must be dry farmed; 3 horses, 1 cow, 1 goat, 1 dog, 1 cat, 1 pig, 15 chickens, 1 plow and 1 wagon. He generally plants beans, corn, cane and oats in May and millet in June.

The last year he made a good crop was in 1929. At present he is supported mainly by working for the Works Projects Administration.

Canuto Lopez

Canuto Lopez, a tall slim man aged 71, differs from most Manzaneños of his age group since he spent most of his life as a day laborer rather than being an independent farmer, livestock raiser or freighter. He went to school for three years and studied only the Spanish language. He can not speak English. His present wife, Luisa, is uneducated.

He was born in Manzano, January 22, 1867, while his wife, almost 30 years younger, was born in Carrizoso, March 24, 1896. His father and mother were born in Tomé and he has three brothers and two sisters living at Manzano. At the age of 22 he married Nemecia Sanchez but she died 20 years later. When he was 54 years old he married Luisa Gomez and now has three children. Her parents, Mr. and Mrs. Narciso Gomez, live in Manzano and receive their support from public welfare programs.

As a young boy he worked for his father herding sheep. After that he used to work from five to six months herding sheep for other owners and made from $20.00 to $30.00 a month. From 1924-1934 he worked as a laborer on a farm belonging to one of the store owners. Canuto worked on the farm for eight hours a day six days a week and made 25 cents an hour or $12.00 a week, saved his money and bought a 16 acre farm. He was 57 years old at the time but could not cultivate the farm because his feet became too bad. He also owns two horses, a small pig and a walking plow. During the past five years he has received surplus commodities and Old Age Assistance.

He and his family live in two rooms of a _jacal_ type of house with two other families, who don't pay rent, and live in the other three rooms. One of their children is in the 4th grade but the oldest boy is too young to attend school. His infant son is very sick with runny eyes and cries all the time. The Lopezes have given him home remedies without success. Canuto claims he has no money for a doctor. He suffers constantly with cold feet which have been that way for 20 years.

Esteben Lopez

He was born in 1862 in La Joya and is 74 years old. The record of his birth was destroyed in a church fire. His father was named Jesús and his mother Josefita. They moved to Manzano when Esteben was a small boy. He never went to school or learned to read or write. When young he married Fernanda Lovato and they had two children who died. Fernanda died in the birth of the third child. Later he married Isabelita Zamora and they had 14 children but only 7 survived. This wife died of stomach trouble. His children are Baltazar (45 years old), Mrs. Ignacio Lopez (41 years old) who lives in Manzano, Mrs. Raimundo Saavedra (40 years old), Maria Freeman who lives in Capitan, and Rebecca Peralta and Bernarda Gomez who live near Jemez.

Esteben made his living as a day laborer and farmer. He sold his farm 17 years ago and has since been unemployed because of arthritis. He and his present wife since then lived in a shanty behind the house of his son Baltazar but now lives with his son in a four room house. The Lopezes receive $8.10 a month from the New Mexico Department of Public Welfare.

Benito Lovato

Benito Lovato is a man 22 years old with a wife 32 years old. This age difference is most unusual at Manzano where the husband generally is older than the wife. They were both born in Manzano. They have one son. Before marriage he worked for the CCC. After marriage in 1939 they lived with his wife's parents. In 1938 they moved into his mother's four room house and farmed her 70 acres for one-third share. He made, however, such poor crops that he was forced to apply for federal relief. Other than personal effects he owns only two horses and one cow.

Tomasita Maestas

Tomasita Maestas, age 85 years, was the oldest women in Manzano. She was born in Tomé in 1855. Her father was born in Tomé and her mother in Punta de Agua. When she was about 10 years old her family moved by oxcart to Las Vegas, trip that took almost a month. Her first husband was Camillo Cordova of Tomé. They had 15 children only one of whom is still alive, a married daughter who lives in Manzano. Her second husband was Reyes Salas who died in 1928. She has a brother living in Punta de Agua and a sister in Carrizozo. Her daughter lost all her crop by hail in 1938. After her second husband died she supported herself by being a housekeeper and doing the laundry for a man in Punta de Agua. Her health is very bad and she is now supported by Old Age Assistance aid.

Antonio Maldonado

Antonio is 22 years old and his wife also 22 years old; both were born in Manzano. He attended school until the fourth grade. Prior to 1935 the total amount he earned working was about $50.00. He worked for a short period on the PWA project building the new school. In 1935 he began receiving public welfare funds. They live in a one room house that his step-father lets them have rent free.

Maximiliana Montano

Maximiliana is a widow, age 65, born in Manzano in 1883. She never went to school and can not read or write. Her father owned a few sheep and goats. She married in 1905 Narciso Montano, a sheepherder who fell in a well in the same year and died of his injuries. They never had any children. She and an adopted niece live in a two room adobe house lent to her by her nephew. The house is very simply furnished having a plank floor, home made rugs, a double iron bed, a hand made table, a chest of drawers, a chair and two hand made benches. She suffers from near sightedness and arthritis. At the time of the interview she was combing wool given by a neighbor to make a quilt.

Frank Morales

Frank Morales is 25 years old and his wife 22; both were born in Manzano. He has a brother and sister living in Mountainair and another in a CCC camp while a sister lives in Manzano. He completed one year of high school and his wife two of high school in Mountainair.

Before he was married he worked on his father's farm. He now cultivates 14 acres of 119 acres of his farm north of Manzano where they live in a one room house in the summer. In Manzano they live the rest of the year in a four room house. He also owns 5 horses, 10 chickens, 1 lister, 1 cultivator, 1 wagon and 1 plow. His crops failed in 1934 and he was forced to apply for federal relief. He is in good health while that of his wife is bad.

Canuto Montano

Canuto, 70 years old, was born in Tomé in 1868 but his parents moved to Manzano when he was only one month old. He went to the local grade school but never learned how to speak English. In 1886 he married Cruzita Gonzales and they had 12 children. She died in childbirth 27 years ago. He then married Leonarda Jaramillo and they had 13 children.

He has been a farmer, woodhauler, and day laborer all his life. Canuto owns 89 acres of land with 40 acres cultivated. In 1936 there was a crop failure. Livestock owned includes 2 horses, 9 goats, and 14 chickens. He has a bad scar that he received in a dance hall fracas 30 years ago.

Juan Romero

Juan Romero, age 28, like many Manzaneños has had a career as an unsuccessful farmer, a day laborer, and finally a relief worker. He and his wife, age 26, were born in Manzano and have three boys and one girl. They live in a two room jacal with meager furnishings. He worked as a farmer until 1937 but had very poor crops. From December 1937 to August 1938 he worked for the PWA at the Manzano School. Then he obtained a laborer's job at Conchas Dam until October. For several weeks he worked as a day laborer in Encino. In 1939 he began working once more for the PWA.

Liandra Romero

Liandra is 86 years old and was born in Manzano in 1852. She can not speak English. Although she is losing her memory she provided much information on the history of Manzano.

Serafico Romero

Among the older men at Manzano Serafico Romero is one of the best educated. He, age 63, was born in 1873 and his wife was born in San Miguel. He came to Manzano at the age of 23. They have a son who is a school teacher and a daughter living with them. Also in their four room house is a grandson seven years old.

He completed the eighth grade and obtained a teaching certificate. He taught off and on. He lost his certificate when New Mexico required a higher education. He owns 100 acres of land of which only 4 can be irrigated. In these irrigated acres he plants alfalfa. Serafico also owns four cows, six horses, six chickens, a two row lister, a one row cultivator, a disc harrow, a mower, a rake, a go-devil and a two section harrow. There was a crop failure in 1934 and he was forced to apply for relief the next year. He is a devout Catholic and active in community affairs. His wife has heart trouble.

Victoriano Romero

Victoriano Romero, age 73 years, was born in 1865 in Manzano. He is small, has blue eyes, gray hair and a moustache. His father was a farmer who owned a few sheep. When a young man Victoriano worked as a sheepherder in Socorro and Lincoln Counties. Later he worked as a farmer and day laborer and a sheepherder during the lambing season. He never attended school or learned to read or write. He married Francesca

Sanchez and had two children both of whom are still living. She left him after 15 years for another man. She left this man in turn for another. Juan is a son living in Mountainair and his daughter, Mrs. Gilberto Martinez, lives in Estancia. He has four grandchildren in Estancia and three in Mountainair.

He lives in a three room adobe house furnished rent free by his daughter. The house is in good condition but rather dirty. On the walls is wallpaper and the house is furnished with a white painted iron bed. He owns 16 acres of which 8 are planted in corn and beans. He also receives aid from the Old Age Assistance program. Owed is $54.00 to Tabet's store and $110 to the Farm Security Administration.

José de la Paz Salas

Salas, age 81 years, was born in Chato in 1857. He first married Severa Trujillo in Belen in 1887 and had a son who still lives there. She died after nine years and he married Flauda Chavez of Belen and she died in 1923. They had no children. He is now living with the Serna family in a three room house and is supported by the Aid-to-the-Blind program, having one blind eye and a cataract in the other. He also lived for a few years in Belen with his son, Simon, age 46. He has had a varied work experience given below:

```
1880-1887 - farmed near Belen
1887-1889 - herded sheep at Manzano for $20.00 a month and room and board
1890-1901 - worked for railroad for $30.00 a month
1902-1905 - herded sheep for Fred Scholle of Belen for $20.00 a month
1906-1915 - did odd jobs at Manzano such as plastering for $20.00 a month
1916-1923 - worked irregularly for Santa Fe Railroad for $30.00 a month
1924 - herded sheep again for Fred Scholle but had to quit because of
failing eyesight
```

Refugia Sanchez

She, age 39, was born in Manzano in 1899. Her parents were Silvero and Ramoncita Romero Vigil. Refugia can read, write and speak English. She married Filimeno Sanchez in 1915 but he died in 1937. Filimeno was the son of Rosa Sanchez and one of the Indian slaves, Eugenio Sanchez, who belonged to the patrón Filimeno Sanchez. Her husband was educated in the Indian school near Capitan. He earned his living as a farmer and sheepherder. When dying he asked Refugia to place a gold earring on his forehead since it was a local belief that by so doing a hemorrhage could be stopped. She has three sons and one daughter. One of her sons went to high school in Mountainair. Refugia lives in an adobe house worth about $100.00 and owns two horses and two pigs. Her house is very clean and furnished with three carved wooden beds. Outside is a small garden.

Manuel Sedillo

Manuel, age 61 years, was born in Manzano in 1877. His parents owned a small farm and a few sheep. He has been a farmer all his life. When young he was injured by a run-away horse and has suffered as a result neck trouble the rest of his life. He is now too blind to work.

He married Francesita Aragon in 1906 and she died in 1918. They had one son who is in a CCC camp. He then married Juanita Chavez of Tajique in 1924. His wife completed grammar school and speaks good English. Juanita was first married to a Mr. Baca who ran a general store in Estancia. He died in 1918.

Manuel owns 30 acres with 20 under cultivation, 2 old horses, 1 cow, 1 calf, 1 wagon, 1 lister, 1 cultivator and 1 go-devil, total property valued at $200. His debts are $229. In 1932 he barely made expenses on his farm while in 1933 he worked for McDonald and Walter of Mountainair. In 1934 he planted 20 acres but had almost complete crop failure and made only 15 sacks of beans.

Max Sedillo

Max, age 40, was born in Manzano in 1899 and is married to Felicita, who was also born in Manzano. He has two boys, Juan José (born in 1936) and Coldendo (1937). They live in a four room house with his mother who owns the house. The mother receives Old Age Assistance. Two of Max's brothers live in Manzano and another in Estancia. His sister lives on a ranch near Torreón.

In 1920 he worked for the Santa Fe Railroad in Estancia. Afterwards, although his health was not good, he began earning his living as a farmer, moving back to Manzano in 1930. Max owns 120 acres of land, 8 of which are cultivated. He also owns two horses, one pig, one lister, one wagon and one cultivator. There were good crops in 1932 and 1933 but since then there has been little yield. He looks down on his fellow Manzaneños who work on relief projects, calling them trouble makers who are always complaining about not receiving their share of relief funds.

Felecita Sedillo

Felecita, age 72, was born in Manzano in 1866 and lived there all her life. Her parents were Antonio Sedillo and Felecita Sanchez who also were born and lived in Manzano. Her brother, Narciso Gomez, and her sister, Dolores Gomez, live in Manzano and her other brother, Poncilano Sanchez, lives in Mountainair. Her education consists of the third grade. She married Antonio Sedillo in 1882 but he died in 1923. They had three children, Max, Frank and Melton, who live in Manzano. Her husband used to farm and after he died Max took care of her until he got married. She lives in two rooms of a four room adobe house which she owns and her son, in the other rooms. The house is very clean and she owns a sewing machine. She still owes $16.00 to Severo Lopez for the house. In religion she is a devout Catholic. Her health is bad.

José Sigala

José Sigalas's grandfather on his father's side carried mail from Chihuahua to Santa Fe in an eight-mule stage coach. His father was named Lorenzo and was born in Mexico. Lorenzo came in an oxcart carrying the machinery for the first sawmill to the Estancia Valley where it was installed near Eastview. The machinery was bought in Trinidad in 1880. He was first married in Mexico but his wife died and the father then came to Chato and married Jose's wife. His mother's father was a full-blooded Indian named José Antonio Silva. This Indian wore his hair long and had a red band tied around his head. His mother's mother was a Spanish woman named Concepción. One time when Concepción was making sopapillas an Indian came to her window and asked for some. She threw hot grease in his face which is reported to have killed him. The house had very small windows with a bar running through the middle. The door was made of one piece of wood and was hinged on the top and bottom with wooden knobs.

Florentino Turrieta

Florentino Turrieta is the oldest man in Manzano and was born in 1845. When interviewed in 1938 he was 93 and had almost lost his memory. He is a tall, thin man with a full growth of hair, a small beard and a moustache. His father was Juan José Turrieta and his mother, Brujida Carnero. His father was the great uncle of the wife of Lucas Zamora, another Manzano informant. The father was killed by Indians in the Manzano Mountains. Turrieta Canyon was named in his honor. Florentino has one sister, 75 years old, who lives in Casa Colorado. He still remembers Indians coming to Manzano. The only buffalo he ever saw was near Pinos Wells. When asked about the people he knew at Manzano when he was young he said he couldn't remember since the priest had thrown all the records away.

He married Manuelita Lucero of Manzano and they have 7 children. They live in a four room house belonging to one of their daughters. In the house is one son, Enecleto (61 years old) who has a back injury and can not work and Valeriano (44 years old) who is nearly blind from a wood chip flying in his eye when he was cutting logs in a sawmill.

He earned most of his living as a farmer and sheepherder but the last time he worked was in 1923 when he picked cotton in Texas. At present he is partially supported by the Old Age Assistance program. He now spends most of his time sleeping or sitting in a chair smoking. Smoking is so important to him that he said the only thing he wanted now was to get enough tobacco to smoke all day.

Max Zamora

Max is a 65 year old man who is well informed on local customs and folklore. Although he believes that witches might have existed in the past, during the time of King Solomon in particular but they no longer are present in the local area. It is possible, however, that they hang around Santa Fe. He is married and can speak a little English. He is a Republican and blames the fact that he has been unemployed for the last 18 months on politics.

The Brazfield Family

The founder of the Brazfield family in Manzano was Dewey, an Anglo-American born in Oklahoma City. He came to Torrance County and married a Spanish-American women. They had three sons by his first marriage. He was killed in an automobile accident 1928 near 4 Mile Corner and his oldest son, Blain, married his step-mother. The son, Alan was born in 1910 and moved to Manzano about 15 years ago where he married Emilia LaJeunese and they had three children, Opal, Claude and Dewey. Alan, a Baptist, has been blind since birth. Blain, 24 years old, is married and has two children. He has a broken down car and supports his two small children and his 2 small half-brothers and a half sister. The brother Eugene, age 21, married a Spanish-American woman of Manzano and is willing to give Alan a home.

The LaJuenese Family

In Manzano is the LaJuenese family of mixed French and Spanish-American descent. The founder was Dositeo born in Taos in 1875 and his wife born in San Geronimo. Dositeo is set apart from the other Manzaneños by his blue eyes. His brother, Silviano, who is the Justice of Peace at Manzano was born in San Fernando in 1878 and his wife in Manzano in 1885. Dositeo has a boy (12 years), a boy (11) and a girl (16). Silviano has three sons and two daughters. Dositeo came to Manzano 30 years ago and lives on a 120 acre farm to the west of Manzano in hilly land with a fertile valley which produces good crops when there is sufficient rain. He also owns 8 horses, 5 cows, 19 sheep, 147 goats, 1 pig, 30 chickens and a 3 room house. Because of crop failure he is now working for the WPA. His wife has tuberculosis. His daughter is married to Blain Brazfield and he has a son in the CCC.

His income record for last 8 years is given below:

1931- made a good corn crop, sold 5 calves for total of $110.00 and 100 goats for $100.00.
1932 -fairly good crop, 300 bushels of corn.
1933-1938 -almost complete crop failure because of droughts and his livestock almost starved to death in 1935 as well as beetles devoured his beans in the same year.

APPENDIX XVI

TABET'S GENERAL STORE

Tabet's general store was founded in the last century by Tenos Tabet. At present it is owned and operated by John Tabet and his two sons, George and Francis. It is a large stone building facing east on the west side of the square.

According to John Tabet the store carries the following merchandize:

Food with a rapid to medium turnover

Bulk pinto beans
Canned coffee
Canned corn
Canned corn beef
Canned grapes
Canned mackerel
Canned milk
Canned peaches
Canned pears
Canned peas
Canned pineapple
Canned pork and beans
Canned salmon
Canned sardines
Canned spinach
Canned tomatoes

Canned vienna sausages
Candy
Coffee beans
Corn Flakes
Flour
Jelly: cherry, grape,
    peach, pear, pineapple
Lard
Macaroni
Oatmeal
Onions
Potatoes
Salt
Syrup
Vermicelli

Food sold in minor quantities

Bread (usually eat home-made tortillas)
Catsup
Canned oysters
Crackers
Dried fruits: peaches and prunes

Peanuts
Pickles
Potted meats
Raisins
Rice

Common food at Anglo-American Stores, absent at Manzano

Cocoa
Chile peppers
Cooked cereals other than oatmeal
Fresh fruits

Fresh meats
Fresh milk
Soda pop
Tea

230

Fresh vegetables

Tobacco

Tobacco sacks (very popular) in order of popularity
    R.J.R., Our Advertizer
    Golden Grain
    Bull Durham
Canned Tobacco
    Union Leader
    Prince Albert
Prefabricated cigarettes (very popular) in order of popularity
    Camels
    Chesterfields
    Lucky Strikes
    Wings
Chewing Tobacco
    Star
    Days Work
Cigars (not popular), carries Perfect brand
Twist tobacco, carries Granger Twist

Soap

    Proctor and Gamble, Crystal White, Peter Pan, Hollywood, Creme
    Oil, Klex, Bouquet, Super Suds, Dutch Cleanser and Palmolive

Medicines, cosmetics, etc.

Alum	Epsom Salts
Antiseptics	Ex Lax
Baby pacifiers	Face powder
Buttons	Liniment
Cold tablets	Lip stick
Cotton	Rouge
Cough medicine	Tooth Paste
Dysentery medicine	

Hardware

Axes	Kerosene
Bolts and screws	Lamps, kerosene
Brooms	Kerosene
Can openers	Machine oil
Carriage bolts	Marbles
Coffee pots (blue-enameled and iron)	Needles, phonograph
Coffee grinders (wood)	Needles, sewing
Combs	Neats Foot Oil
Dust pans	Screws
Friction tape	Turpentine
Horse shoes and collar pads	

Clothing

Dresses, cotton print and rarely silk	Neckties
Garters, (rarely sold)	Pants, blue denim

Hats, cowboy, felt, and straw	Shoes, dress and work
Lingerie	Sweaters
Neckties	Underwear
Overalls	

Comments on items purchased

A cross section of Manzano's adaptation to Anglo-American culture is revealed in the types of items that are purchased in the stores vs. those made at home or raised in the gardens. The purchased items are limited to those things that reflect the life of livestock raisers, farmers, and employment on government relief projects. While objects for horses and wagons are sold locally no automobile parts are stocked in the store. Patent medicines are available for common illness. Clothing sold reflects the rural life. Cosmetics, lingerie, print and silk dresses are bought by younger women who have abandoned the severe traditional black clothing and shoes of the elders. The lack of electricity is revealed in the sale of kerosene lamps. No longer are pots, soap, brooms and agricultural tools made at home and their place is taken by commercial items. Phonograph needles are available. Fresh vegetables, fruits and meat are locally raised while tortillas are made at home.

MANZANO FAMILY NAMES

A rough measure of the mobility and disappearance of families is revealed in the history of family names. In the petition for a land grant of December 24, 1829, are the signatures of 119 individuals in addition to that of the chief signature of Juan José Sanchez. In the group were 44 family names that included these names of families containing more than five signatures: Torres (14), Sanchez (11), Chavez (10), Montoya (8), Sedillo (7), Garcia (5), Luera (5), Otero (5) and Perea (5). Several of these names are shared with the early immigrants to the central Rio Grande Valley which was the major place of emigration to Manzano. Among these names are Baca, Chavez, Garcia, Otero, Padilla, Sedillo and Velasquez (Espinosa and Chavez, no date:139-187). In addition, several names are those of the migrants to New Mexico during the Colonial Period. For example, the Baca family can be traced to Bernardo José Baca to whom De Vargas granted the Pueblo Viejo land at La Cienega, in 1701. The Garcia family can be traced to José Garcia Jurado who joined the 1893 colonists under De Vargas while the founder of the Chavez family in New Mexico was Pedro Duran y Chavez who joined the original Oñate colony at San Gabriel in 1600. The Sanchez family can be traced to Pedro Sanchez, a soldier in the Coronado Expedition of 1540. Pedro Cedillo de Rojas, a member of the De Vargas reconquest of 1698, was the founder of the Sedillo family. The Torres family traces its ancestry to Cristobal Torres who was given a Spanish land grant near the old pueblo of Chamal.

Of the 44 different names in the Grant petition 36 were represented by only one or two names. In addition, the average number of people with the same names was five petitioners. Some of the individuals with the same name may have not been related since most of the names of the grant petitioners are common names throughout New Mexico. However, the fact that they all lived in the small area of the central Rio Grande Valley probably indicates that these individuals were related. Examining these data it would appear that the majority of settlers to Manzano were single family groups plus some single individuals or a group of two or more brothers. In this group were four single women listed as household heads. Such a pattern of migrants is characteristic of pioneer settlements. In addition, the fact that 36 families were represented probably indicates that families of all sizes migrated to Manzano. In addition, that four single women signed the petition as household heads indicates the vast predominance of married couples that came to Manzano.

A comparison of the 120 names shared in the grant petitioners with those of 44 different names of the registered voters in 1938, a period extending over 110 years, reveals only 21 names in common or slightly less than half. Thus over half of the original names had disappeared by families moving away or lacking male heirs. These facts also suggest than there were no more family groups in Manzano than there were in the original settlement. Yet there were twice the number of household heads, being 120 in 1829 and 209 in 1938. In other words the size of the families had about doubled. In addition, there were 8 Anglo-American heads in the Manzano precinct as well as 4 Syrians families.

APPENDIX XVIII

THE FARM OF EUGENIO GONZALES

One of the more successful farming operations is that of Eugenio Gonzales near the Quarai Indian ruins. He owns 130 acres on which is a garden irrigated by a small pond that has its source in a nearby spring. A windmill pumps the water from the pond into the garden. Even a dry year such as 1938 the spring still produces enough water for the garden. During this year the garden produced over 200 heads of cabbage as well as chile, tomatoes, beets, carrots, watermelons and squash. In 1939 he planted his garden on April 18th and 19th. Several acres of alfalfa are also irrigated from the pond.

Corn, cane and beans are dry farmed and he does lose these crops during droughts. The crops were planted with an automatic planter on April 28 to May 2nd, 1939. It takes approximately 5 pounds of corn, 15 pounds of beans and 20 pounds of cane to plant his field. The ground is too hard for growing potatoes but nearby Frank Vallejos is able to plant this crop. At one time Gonzales planted tobacco and it now comes up wild. There is also a small orchard of wild plums. He also has one domesticated tree that produces large plums. There was at one time a peach tree but it died. A small proportion of Gonzales's land has juniper and pinyon trees. He has had enough success with agriculture that he has not been forced to go to work on relief projects.

ETHNOBOTANICAL DATA AND LOCAL MEDICINES*

Cachana: _Liastris_ sp., a herb that is burnt as a cure for deafness.

Cachania: unidentified, a wild herb that is given to sick babies.

Calabazilla: _Cucurbita foetidissima_, the wild gourd is used for a laxative. It is boiled in water for three days and let stand. This water is also placed in a pan in a room since its smell drives away insects.

Camote: _Peteria_ sp., wild plant with roots good to eat as soon as taken from the ground.

Cedro: _Juniperus scopulorum Serg._, the local juniper tree; the bows are boiled in water which is then applied to the body for colds, influenza, and pneumonia.

Contrayerba: _Kallstroemia brachystylis_, a herb used to heal wounds.

Chimaja: _Aulospermun purpureum_ or _Cymopterus purpureus_ S. Watts, wild herb used to flavor brandy.

Chile, green: _Capsicum annuum_, used as a cure for gum disease.

Culantro: _Coriandrum sativum_ L. [coriander], leaves and seeds boiled in water and given to newborn babies.

Damiana: _Turnera humifusa_ (Presl), Endlich or _Crysactinia mexicana_ Grey, herb used for stomach trouble and to strengthen blood.

Garrambullo: _Opuntia leptocaulis_, prickly pear fruit used for food and jelly.

Inmortal: _Asclepiodora decumbens_ Nutt. F., herb used for nasal congestion.

Mariola: _Artemisia rhizomata_ A Nels., a sage boiled in water for stomach trouble.

Moradilla: _Verbena ambrosiaefolia_ Rydb., boiled in water for use as a relief from arthritis.

Oshá: _Linguisticum Porteri_ Coult. and Rose, herb boiled for stomach trouble.

Oregano: <u>Monarda</u> <u>menthaefolia</u> Graham [horsemint], a spice cultivated to give flavor to chile.

Palmilla de Amole: a local yucca sp., the root of which is used for washing hair and clothes.

Palo Duro: <u>Cercoparpus</u> <u>montanus</u> Raf., a perennial bush the berries of which are eaten by deer; leaves are boiled in water; the water is rubbed on body for a skin disease called <u>lepera</u>.

Palo Amarillo: <u>Berberis</u> <u>fremontii</u> Torr, large yellow-colored bush; the wood is boiled in water to get a brown dye for deerskins.

Ponga: unidentified, a mushroom that is dried, powdered and placed in ear for earache.

Punche Mexicana: <u>Nicotiana</u> sp., a locally cultivated tobacco used for cuts, wounds and for smoking.

Quilite: <u>Amaranthis</u> sp. [lambsquarter], leaves eaten as greens.

Rosa de Castilla: <u>Rosa</u> <u>centifolia</u> ?, flowers are dried and powdered. They are then mixed with cold water and drunk for stomach trouble.

Yerba Buena: <u>Mentha</u> <u>spicata</u> L. [spearmint], used in steam for pregnant women.

Yerba de Agua: unidentified, small water plants, leaves boiled on water and mixed with sugar. It is drunk in morning and evening for swelling of the testicles.

Yerba de la Víbora: <u>Gutierrezia</u> <u>tenuis</u> Greene, herb boiled in water for boils

*Identification based upon similarities of Spanish names in the descriptions given of Hispano-American medicinal plants by Ford (1975).

238

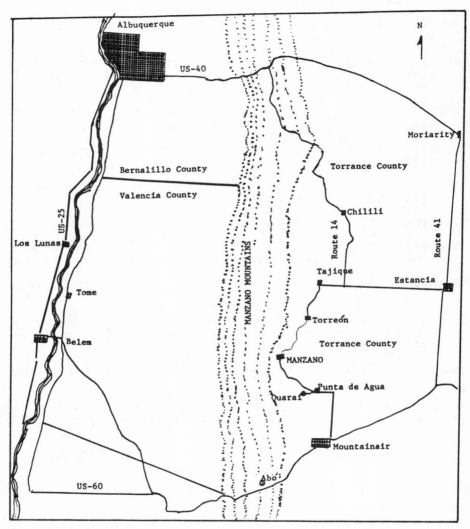

LOCATION OF MANZANO

FIGURE I

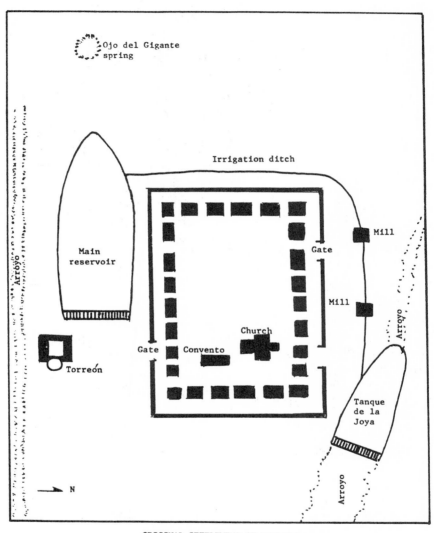

ORIGINAL SETTLEMENT OF MANZANO
(from sketch by Lucas Zamora)

FIGURE II

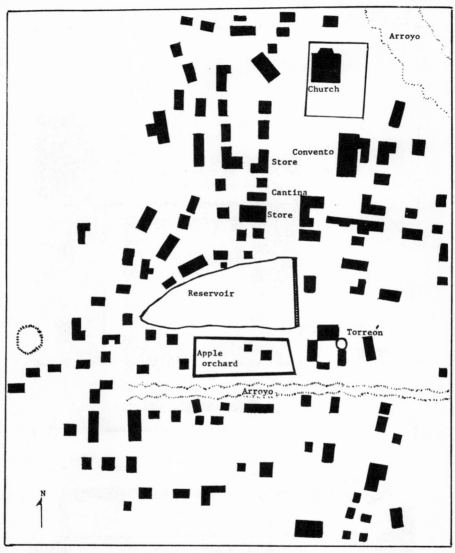

MANZANO, 1939
FIGURE III

Figure IV: The spring,
Ojo del Gigante

Figure V: The school building

Figure VI: The church

Figure VII: The convento

Figure VIII: The torreón

Figure IX: The communal graveyard

Figure X: The reservoir

Figure XI: Mr. and
Mrs. Julian Sanchez

Figure XII: Stone house

Figure XIII: Jacal type of house

Figure XIV: Multiple house

Figure XV: Multiple house

Figure XVI: Multiple house

Figure XVII: Apple orchard

Figure XVIII: Corn field

Figure XIX: New reservoir under construction

Figure XX: Tabet's general store

Figure XXI: Fiesta of Nuestra Senora de Dolores

Figure XXII: Ceremony of Una Visita